LIVING IN MY SISTER'S SHADOW

A PERSPECTIVE ON ADDICTION, LOSS AND WHAT IT MEANS TO MOVE ON

Amanda Bourque

Sober and Beyond

Tampa, FL

DEDICATION

To **Jenna**, my baby sister. You came crashing into my life, rearranged everything and left just as quickly. We survived childhood by leaning on each other. I only made it out because of you. I only made something of myself because of you. Even after your death, I still strive to be an example for you. You will forever be my guiding light.

To **Kelly Riley**. You led me down the path of writing this book. You stood beside me the entire time and encouraged me to grow, expand, and overcome personal blockages. Thank you for following your instincts and offering me such immeasurable support.

To all **those affected by addiction**. The suffering is immense, and the wound is deep. Though the pain may sometimes be insufferable, all-consuming or ceaseless, it does get easier. I promise you. There is light. There is a purpose.

ISBN: 979-8-9921861-0-9 (Paperback)

ISBN: 979-8-9921861-1-6 (Hardcover)

ISBN: 979-8-9921861-2-3 (E-book)

Library of Congress Control Number: 2025904981

This memoir is a truthful recollection of actual events in the author's life. Some conversations have been recreated and/or supplemented. The names and details of some individuals have been changed to respect their privacy.

First printing edition 2025

Sober and Beyond

Tampa, FL

www.soberandbeyond.com

TABLE OF CONTENTS

INTRODUCTION

The overdose death of my younger sister left me devastated and wondering about my own existence. Navigating her active addiction, processing her death, grieving, and then moving on with my own life was a scary, complicated and a heartbreaking experience. I felt alone, angry and guilty for the majority of it.

Regardless of what I did or didn't do, I felt like I was doing the wrong thing. Each time I reached out for help it was met with a discouraging and inadequate response. I never felt supported, heard, or understood during the entire situation.

Most people would say nothing at all. Instead, they would just look at me with a sad expression on their face as if they wanted to say something but didn't want to risk being the bearer of bad news.

Self-care? Boundaries? My sister was going to die. My sister was sucking all the life out of me. I was frantic and afraid of what her death would mean for me.

I needed to do anything and everything possible to prevent that from happening. Yet, no one understood or could give me actionable steps to ensure her safety.

I felt all alone on my mission to save her. I trudged through darkness and barely survived the weight of her life choices. Nothing I did for her ever worked and the realization of that left me hopeless and feeling like a failure as an older sister.

Her death was the worst thing I have ever experienced. No pain had ever come close to the grief and depression of losing Jenna. I almost didn't make it out of the anguish. I almost disintegrated into it.

The guilt and anger of her death were paralyzing and turned me into a stranger. I did things that made me feel like I was losing control or had already lost it.

As I began to come out from under my sister's shadow, I had to relearn who I was as a changed person. What life meant to me now that Jenna was gone, and how to live without her.

I got certified as an addiction recovery coach and began volunteering at an addiction rehabilitation center. I also participated in local sober events and began sharing my story.

Writing about my experience enables me to offer the world insight, understanding and compassion for anyone in a similar situation. I am unafraid of being the bearer of bad news and openly expressing every aspect of the journey. Every moment of rage. Every moment of failure. Every moment of despair.

No one should be alone during such intense and life altering experiences. This book, my story, ensures that you will no longer be alone.

CHAPTER ONE

.·.

"Don't ever be ashamed of loving the strange things that make your weird little heart happy."
Elizabeth Gilbert

The phone call that changed my life was the one that ended my world. It permanently altered everything about how I perceived reality. It was the moment I learned that my younger sister, Jenna, had died from an overdose.

The news took my breath away and left me collapsed on the floor, wailing like an infant. Jenna was everything to me.

We endured a terribly abusive childhood, and she was the only person I could confide in, the only one who truly understood what was happening and how it felt. Often, we would comfort each other in the middle of the night, taking turns being the one crying and the one consoling.

The pain we suffered was immeasurable, yet we experienced it together. Through the isolation of a traumatic childhood, Jenna was the one person who made me feel love and connected to life. She gave me a reason to keep going.

And now, here I was, sprawled on the kitchen floor, crying as if my own life had ended. In many ways, it had.

My life, as I knew it, ended the moment she died. Jenna had been my reason to live, and without her, I could only imagine reasons not to.

My head spun from the news of her death. I had an endless number of questions but no capacity to voice them. The room seemed to warp and spin around me, making me feel as though I were hallucinating. My breathing shortened into hurried gasps as my entire world came crashing down.

My heart shattered, and it felt as though my soul had vacated my body. The weight of it all was unbearable, a reality I simply couldn't accept.

Jenna had been too monumental to just leave. She was my purpose for living. It was impossible to comprehend that she was gone so quickly, so suddenly. How could she leave without even saying goodbye?

Life had started out awful, yes, but somehow, I had managed to make something out of nothing. I built a life where my fantasies of love, family, and fulfillment had all come true. I had everything I ever wanted. And yet, Jenna still died. Where did it all go wrong?

To find that out, we need to back up to how life was before Jenna died. Before I even knew she had an addiction. When life was good, and I was happy.

I woke up as usual, to the sound of an alarm clock buzzing in my ear. I turned it off, swung my legs over the side of the bed, and placed them on the cold concrete floor.

Taking a moment, I looked around. The floor was grey; the walls were pale pink, uneven, and painted as though by a child. A small shelf was built into a carved-out hole in the wall.

Was I still dreaming? I rubbed my eyes and shook my shoulders to be sure. Nope, not dreaming.

Light shone through the gap beneath my closed bedroom door. After one long exhale, I stood up and prepared to start the day.

Approaching the door, I grabbed the handle, turned it, and pulled it open, almost holding my breath as I did so. Opening that door felt like stepping into an alternate reality.

The sun beamed down on my face with full force. People bustled around in all directions, each seemingly aware of their task and intent on completing it as quickly as possible. People came and went from the shower and toilet rooms.

Someone gathered clothes to wash by the river. Another tended to a fire beneath a massive pot, heating water for showers.

Children ran chaotically, filled with excitement as they prepared for school or a day of freedom. Meanwhile, a few women rolled out dough for roti, while another prepared spices and vegetables for curry.

Every morning, opening my bedroom door overwhelmed my senses. The sights, sounds, smells, and textures seemed amplified to a ten. It was particularly jarring when I wasn't feeling well.

Normally, I'm a quiet-morning person, the type who needs an hour of silence before facing the world. So that my mind could grasp that the dream-state was over, and reality had begun. Yet, here in Hampi, India, that wasn't an option.

Honestly, I'm pretty sure peace and quiet are illegal in India or at least it feels that way. Regardless, I wouldn't trade this for anything. I love living in India. I love being in this village.

After more than ten months here, I couldn't be happier. My soul feels at ease. I feel like I have a family and finally belong somewhere. It's an incredible experience, one I've never had before.

Once I was finished brushing my teeth and using the toilet, I returned to my room to change into exercise clothes.

Grabbing my jump rope, I made my way to the main room and climbed the ladder to the rooftop.

Every house here has a rooftop, and it's such a fun space to hang out. Since the village is small and deeply traditional, I prefer exercising on the rooftop.

It's less intrusive for them and provides me with privacy and a breathtaking view of the surrounding streets.

The roads are dirt and only accessible by motorcycle, rickshaw, bicycle, or walking. Cars stop at the main entrance, making the interior quiet, safe, and unique.

From the rooftop, I could see the streets and shortcut paths as people passed through the area. Small children ran and played while adults set out to complete their morning tasks.

In the distance, I could see the banana fields, their vibrant green contrasting with the gray and brown boulders that defined Hampi's unique beauty.

With my phone as a timer and for music, I began my jump rope routine. I've gotten good at it, forty minutes without stopping or messing up.

It's my main cardio activity, one that clears my mind or lets me drift off and dissociate. Jumping regularly has significantly improved my stamina, and now I can't start the day without it.

Initially, I came to sight-see for a few days and now

it seemed as though I was living here. Doing normal, mundane tasks and assimilating into the community.

I originally had plans to backpack through Europe, yet India did what it has done before.

It has this way of grasping me. Luring me into staying longer than planned or going off on unexpected adventures.

I've visited the country several times before and it's always the same. India gives me the experience that it wants, not the one that I had planned. I've learned to surrender to its will which makes each trip unique and enthralling.

After finishing my exercise, I headed to the shower room, a narrow, tiled space with just a showerhead, a drain, and cold water.

If I wanted warm water, I'd have to heat it over an open fire, then carry it to the shower room and use a cup to bathe. I never go through that effort; cold water is better for the body anyway.

Afterward, I changed into my outfit for the day: black leggings and a long pink shirt that fell to my mid-thigh.

It was 8:30 AM and time to head to the river. I grabbed a small purse for essentials; money, Chapstick, sunscreen, and my phone and set out.

As a foreigner living in Hampi, I'm something of a local celebrity. People stop to say hello, ask how my day is going, or inquire about what I ate for breakfast.

Sometimes, they just wave or silently stare. It took time to adjust to the constant attention, but now I feel a bit disappointed if no one asks for a photo with me.

If I return from the town with a shopping bag, everyone insists on peeking inside. It's impossible to evade their curiosity; they'll grab the bag, inspect its contents, and even ask for something to share.

I once had a friend send me a letter to the village. It was a lazy afternoon, and a small child ran up to me with an open and torn envelope, speaking in indecipherable English. The child was excited, so I smiled and played along.

After a few moments she handed me the envelope. My eyes glanced down at the text and focused on the perfectly written English. It was my letter. I was initially upset however; Indians can't help themselves sometimes and it's mostly innocent.

To this day I have no idea if the person sent any money. Hopefully they didn't. If they did, hopefully it was spent with glee. The curiosity here is so extreme that I'm convinced everyone must have been cats in a past life.

While the attention can be exhausting on the days when I crave solitude, for the most part, I enjoy the stark contrast to life in the US. How can you ever feel lonely when you're surrounded by great company? Like it or not, the village will be your companion.

Turning down the dirt road, my feet were already grubby from the combination of loose dirt and open sandals. To be honest, I enjoy it, it reminds me of childhood, playing outside all day without a care. Societal pressures are different. Being a little dirty is normal, and no one minds.

Here in South India, it's common to walk barefoot, and the men even find it attractive. Women walk gracefully with bare feet, their silver anklets chiming with each step. You have to tread carefully to avoid rocks, scorpions, spit, or cow dung.

I've tried walking barefoot a few times. It feels freeing, and the locals love it when I embrace their lifestyle.

When walking barefoot I only ever notice the ground. I'm not interested in the sensation of stepping into a massive pile of cow dung that seemingly litters the roads, paths, fields. Well, the entire area. Since I have sandals on today, I only needed to be half as vigilant about cow dung.

On my way to the river, I stopped at the local chai stand. It's not the best chai, but the vendor is kind. He speaks a little English and is always happy to see me.

I got my usual small cup of chai and sipped it slowly, watching life pass by at the main bus stop.

Life whizzes past as I witness it's dance. I'm always entertained watching people come and go, packages being delivered and shipped, children and teenagers getting on and off buses, and people rushing to get home or catch the next bus.

I enjoy sipping chai and observing the hustle at Hampi's bus stop. I can't help but fall in love with the simplicity of life here.

The people are open and loving and there seems to be a sort of magic in the air. I have been traveling for the past few years so perhaps my body craves the peacefulness of a small village.

Either way, I have never felt connected to much of anything before. I've always felt like an outsider or a wanderer.

I never allowed myself to build those types of bonds because it never felt safe. As though it would be ripped away from me at the exact moment that I relaxed.

To prevent disappointment and pain I prevented relationships. I had my younger sister, Jenna, and a flimsy tie to our mother, Mother Mary. Even those core connections were unsteady and unpredictable.

After finishing my chai, I continue toward the river, walking along the dirt road while being asked several times by motorcyclists and rickshaw drivers if I need a ride. Small places like this are warm and kind; everyone helps everyone. If you need something, you'll be helped.

I decline the offers for rides because the walk is relaxing, and I want the exercise. As I get closer, the road opens up, revealing more of the river with every stride.

A small peek appears after rounding a corner, a slight glimmer of water behind the green trees and brush. The further I go, the less dense the foliage becomes, and more of the water is revealed.

Parked motorcycles and rickshaws line the edge of the embankment. Monkeys sway in the trees and perch on the embankment's fenced edge.

Some even relax on motorcycle seats. Occasionally, the monkeys get bold and rummage through the pouches on rickshaws and motorcycles, looking for snacks. It's funny to watch, though I'm sure it's not as amusing for the owners.

The monkeys begin by looking around to ensure no one is watching, then swoop in and land on the vehicle. They seem to have a plan, unbuckling or unlatching bags and rummaging through them.

Each item is inspected, and if deemed undesirable, it's tossed to the ground. The monkeys work quickly, sorting through all the bag's contents.

Sometimes they get lucky and find food, retreating immediately with their prize. Other times, they come up empty and move on to another target. Not today, though. Today, they're just hanging out, people-watching and gathering in groups.

I couldn't count the number of times I have seen monkeys rush into corner stores when no one was looking.

They would quickly snatch chips, fruit, crackers or bread and run out. Instantly bounding up a tree, telephone pole or house to enjoy their loot out of harm's way.

I often wonder what monkeys are plotting when they gather like that. If someone told me they were planning to take over the village, I'd believe it.

As I reach the edge of the embankment, I pause to take in the scenery. A metal fence lines the embankment, with massive stone steps leading down to the water's edge.

The stones spread out on either side, opening to the shoreline. Men linger along the riverbank, chatting, snacking, napping, or simply observing.

Several groups of women in brightly colored outfits are stationed at the shallow parts of the river, washing clothes with bars of soap and agitating the fabric on stones.

Some work feverishly, scrubbing the clothes, making them sudsy, then slamming them against the rocks as though they're physically beating out the dirt. Their gold and glass bangles create a rhythmic clinking sound with every movement.

Some women operate assembly-line style, passing each item along to the next person, while others work solo. The final step is always a few more slams against the rocks before the clothes are laid out to dry in the sun.

It's a mesmerizing sight almost like interpretive dance. Watching them, it's hard to believe this is just a household chore. They leave their clothes out to dry and then come back to retrieve them later.

The vibrant colors of the women's clothing, the rhythmic sounds of clinking bangles, lounging monkeys, and resting men are all captivating.

Yet, they're only the backdrop for the real reason I come to the river every morning: to watch the temple elephant being bathed.

Each morning, her keeper brings her to the river for a bath. He scrubs her with a long brush, spending close to an hour cleaning her. It's an intense and fascinating ritual to witness.

Of course, the idea of a lone elephant confined to a village temple her entire life feels cruel. And sometimes, I feel bad for her, imagining the loneliness she might experience.

However, travel has taught me that everyone is free to view the world in their own way. In that freedom, it's important not to interfere with local customs and traditions.

They believe what they believe. Who's to say I'm right and they're wrong or vice versa? It depends on what you see as to how easy this is to adopt.

That said, there are days when the keeper's behavior disturbs me. Occasionally, he jabs her with a training stick that has a metal point, and she cries out in pain.

On those days, I leave the river immediately. I don't condone abuse, but I know I can't change their way of life. In such moments, I'd rather not witness it.

Mostly because I, myself was abused as a child. Watching the abuse of others resurrects an immense experience of sadness and empathy. It's often overwhelming and makes me feel as though I am reliving my childhood.

It's easier for me to walk away or shield myself from witnessing such acts, especially when I have no power to change the situation.

Sitting along the upper shoreline, I take in the scene: women washing clothes, children swimming and playing, men resting and conversing, the elephant being bathed, and monkeys darting from tree to tree.

It's not even 10 AM, and I find myself asking that same question again. I rub my eyes and shake my shoulders, checking to make sure. Nope. Not dreaming. This is my life.

At that moment, I decided something: I'm going to stay here in Hampi. It's the only place I've ever felt like I belong.

It's the only place I've felt loved, accepted, and part of a community. It's the only place where my soul feels at ease. Why would I go back to the US or anywhere else, for that matter? My home is here.

CHAPTER TWO

.˙.

"If there are things you don't like in the world you grew up in, make your own life different."

Dave Thomas

The following weeks were spent figuring out the logistics of my decision to stay. The first priority was finding my own place, a small two-room hut where I could have space to myself.

A place where I could do yoga, take naps, learn to cook on an open fire, and collect water. I had never lived in a small hut alone before, and I knew this would be a great experience.

Since some huts in the village don't have toilets, I needed to ensure mine did. Otherwise, I'd have to carry a small jug of water to the pooping field every morning, like everyone else.

Have you ever seen a field full of people pooping in the morning? It's both comical and surreal, like a parallel reality for Westerners.

I once had an invitation to the pooping field from my friend's sister. She wanted us to walk hand-in-hand to the field so I could accompany her while she did her business. She even wanted her sister-in-law to come along too!

Can you imagine needing an entourage to go poop? I can't even do it in front of a cat or dog. Her name was Maya, and she was truly sweet. I loved her, even if she lured me to my first pooping field.

If I was going to stay in Hampi, I also needed a source of income. I spoke with a few local men to discuss my options, which included working at a restaurant or investing in a small business.

My presence was seen as an asset because it drew in locals and made tourists feel comfortable, a distinct advantage when it came to earning money.

The village only had a handful of restaurant options, so starting a new business with a fresh idea seemed promising. I knew what tourists wanted because I was one.

I thought about opening a smoothie shop,

particularly one that offered protein powder options for the local men. It would be easy to fund and establish, and it would introduce a novelty food option.

Then there was the issue of my visa. I'd need to find a way to stay, either by leaving every six months to re-enter with a fresh stamp or marrying a local man for a more permanent solution.

While I wanted to get married eventually, I didn't want to rush into it. Leaving every six months seemed manageable for now.

The weeks flew by as I planned my next steps, and while it was busy, it was also incredibly exciting. I had finally found a place where I truly belonged.

Feeling like I had family and a community was liberating and emotional. I now understand why people enjoy going home, being with family, and visiting their old neighborhoods.

I couldn't relate to that before. Growing up, my house had been a kind of torture, a hell to endure. Far from anything pleasurable or desirable.

I used to think everyone lived in misery, crying themselves to sleep each night. I never understood why people didn't just give up on life. It wasn't until I visited my friends' homes that I realized it wasn't universal.

It was just my reality. That realization was depressing,

but it also gave me hope that life could be different.

Then came India, and everything changed. From my very first trip, I felt interwoven with its essence. My soul felt at ease the moment I stepped onto the soil.

I had finally found alignment and unity, and I couldn't imagine letting that go. Why should I? I'd waited my entire life to feel this way, to have a home.

Life was good, and everything seemed to be falling into place. I was at peace, at ease, with a heart overflowing with love.

I felt deeply connected to the Universe, to the source of energy that guides us all. That energy stayed with me throughout the day, no matter what mundane or tedious task I was doing.

I often climbed the boulder mountains around the village to watch the sunset. My good friend Akash usually accompanied me.

We had met on my first morning in Hampi, after a long overnight bus ride in an old, bumpy school bus that left me delirious.

When we arrived, the rickshaw drivers swarmed the station, bombarding passengers before they even stepped off the bus. It was chaotic and overwhelming, especially after a sleepless night. As I got off, I locked eyes with a tall, slim man standing behind the crowd of drivers.

It felt like a scene from a movie. The crowd parted, and I found myself walking straight toward him. I didn't know why, but his eyes felt familiar.   They felt safe.

He smirked as I drew closer. He was extraordinarily handsome. He was model material, really, with a strong, defined jawline and the faintest stubble.

I walked right up to him, and his smirk widened into a smile. Even his teeth were perfect. His posture was casual, with no sense of urgency.

In a gentle, smooth voice, he told me to ignore the other rickshaw drivers and mentioned that we could walk to the village in less than two minutes.

I eagerly followed him as he offered to help me find a place to stay. I accepted, and he took me to his aunt's guesthouse.

Akash showed me to my room and then escorted me to the rooftop, where we hung out for a while and talked. He was mellow and had caring eyes.

I felt connected to him from the very moment our eyes locked at the bus station. Akash and I have spent nearly every day together since I arrived.

He helped me find places to eat, buy specific items, and took me to nearby towns. He toured me around the ancient ruins, showed me local shortcuts and scenic views, and even took me on adventures to neighboring areas.

We often ran errands for his family together. He was my best friend, always there for me. I'd call him, and he'd drive up in his rickshaw.

One lazy afternoon by the river, he even taught me how to drive one. Though, he'll tell you that I accidentally took off and he had to jump in and take over.

We enjoyed going for walks along trails that only the locals knew about. We would wander into the dense vegetation and always seemed to end at a lookout point or secluded clearing.

Sometimes we would take naps on warm boulders or wide banana leaves. We were carefree and I felt like a teenager falling in love for the first time.

On one walk in particular, my sandal broke, and I got wedged between a boulder crevice. We giggled the entire time as he comically rescued me and made fun of my insistence to continue onward using only one shoe.

As the months passed, we shared laughter, tears, secrets, and aspirations. Akash always took care of me, and I always felt safe with him. I began to depend on him for not only basic needs but for companionship as well.

Eventually, we grew even closer, sharing kisses and even speaking of marriage. I wanted that. A nice, small life in a tiny village. Where I could disappear into my newfound concept of home.

I was content with him and the world seemed to disappear around us. It felt as though it was just us and I was happy in it. The past didn't exist and the future was the ultimate female fantasy. We get married, have children, grow old, and end our lives together.

After contemplating our plans for the future, we decided to ask his family for permission. Since the majority of marriages in India are arranged, most families are not open to anything other than that.

We knew the probability of rejection was high. Yet, we decided to hope for the best and ask anyway.

Unfortunately, his family didn't approve. Although they welcomed me into their home and enjoyed my company, they were traditional.

Akash was expected to marry an Indian woman through an arrangement, with no exceptions. His mother even threatened to kill herself if we were to proceed without her blessing.

I was a very intense exchange with a lot of anger and tears. Thankfully it wasn't in English, so I had no idea what was said.

We were both heartbroken, but there was no way to fight it. Neither of us were willing to proceed without their blessing. Things were the way they were.

We continued to have a relationship even though it

would never be anything more than that. Maybe we were attempting to slowly taper our sorrow.

As I continued to consider the possibility of marrying a local man for a visa, it felt wrong to imagine anyone but Akash. Yet, it would have to be anyone else but him.

The days, weeks, and months felt like a fever dream. It was hard to believe how drastically my life had transformed. Fulfillment and love replaced the emptiness I once knew.

The gratitude I held in my heart for Hampi was immeasurable. My life felt like a fairytale, my happily ever after. I had finally received it.

Even though figuring out how to permanently stay would be my challenge, I was determined to find a way. It would be the final hurdle in a long journey to contentment.

At least, that is what I thought. I thought my life had settled and that I could finally relax. I was satisfied with a small life, but the Universe had other plans.

Late one night I went to the village internet cafe to check emails and browse the latest news. After scrolling down through my Gmail account, I noticed a familiar name. It was an email from my younger sister, Jenna.

Although we had grown distant since I left the US, she was my only sibling, and I loved her more than anything. She didn't respond much to my emails so seeing her message in my inbox made me feel excited. The message read:

> *Hey,*
>
> *I am really scared right now. I don't know what to do. I have a problem, and I need help. I have an addiction, and I am really scared.*
>
> *Jenna*

CHAPTER THREE

∴

"Here's a rule of life: you don't get to pick what bad things happen to you."

Rory Miller

The initial excitement instantly faded as my stomach tightened into a knot. An addiction? Jenna has always been dramatic, that's just how she operates.

The more dramatic she was, the more attention she received. Because of that, I never took her too seriously. I brushed off most of her grievances because I could never tell if, or when they were genuine.

I assumed most of her actions were nothing more than bids for attention. I love her to death, but we're in our twenties now. When does that childish behavior end?

Don't get me wrong, the strategy worked when we were kids. No matter what was happening, she could refocus all the attention onto herself in an instant. Even now, her methods still work. She gets all the attention and continues to be treated like a child.

There were moments when this dynamic genuinely irritated me, but for the most part, I just rolled my eyes and moved on.

She paid for the attention-seeking in ways I wasn't willing to, and deep down, I knew I'd never play that role myself. Might as well step aside and let the best person hold the position.

I, on the other hand, was the angry one. I refused to accept abuse with a smile. I wouldn't pretend everything was fine or that I wasn't dragged across the room by my hair the night before. Jenna preferred to smile at breakfast and act like nothing happened.

She'd plead with me, practically get on her knees, begging me to pretend everything was okay. Rarely did I oblige. Maybe that's why she was the favorite. She was more agreeable.

As attention-seeking as Jenna could be, this email wasn't like her. I had never heard her identify as an addict or ask for help in such a raw, direct way.

I reread her words several times, letting them sink in.

My gut told me to go to her immediately. I had to find out what was going on.

Even if she was being dramatic, there could still be cause for concern. Maybe she was drinking too much or smoking too much weed. Perhaps she got blackout drunk and woke up somewhere unfamiliar. As her older sister, it was my responsibility to ensure she was okay. If she needed me, I had no choice but to go.

I bought the next ticket out of India, headed for New Hampshire. I had no idea what was going on with Jenna, but I had a feeling of greater uncertainty, almost as if I was being asked to choose between Hampi and her. Of course, I have to choose Jenna. That's not even a consideration. But it's still heartbreaking.

I've been searching all my life for a sense of belonging, and I finally found it. I finally have a family. I finally feel loved and accepted. And now I have to leave? Was it only temporary? What kind of cruelty is that?

It's like, "*Here, take a nibble. A teeny, tiny nibble. Enjoy the sensation. Now, step back and forever fantasize about your teeny, tiny nibble that you will never have again for the rest of your life.*"

Sometimes my life feels like a trick, a dangling carrot that was never meant to be eaten. Is it better to have loved and lost than to have never loved at all?

I'm not sure about that just yet. Right now, I wish I never even had a taste. Something tells me that my goodbyes aren't temporary.

My heart is heavy with pain at the thought of leaving Hampi. I'm obsessed with what I've found here, and I never want to step foot outside it.

I'm insecure that if I leave, even for a moment, I'll never be able to return. Or if I do, things will never be the same. They'll forget about me. Move on with their lives. I'll realize that I loved them more than they loved me.

Leaving the village was one of the hardest things I've ever had to do. I couldn't even say goodbye to everyone. There were some people I avoided so I wouldn't have to do it.

I hate saying goodbye. My throat closes, my chest feels dense, and all I can do is cry. All those beautiful words that can be expressed during a goodbye are lost on me. They remain forever in my mind but never on my lips.

It might seem cruel to not say goodbye to certain people. It might even be offensive. Just know that if I never say goodbye to you, it's because I love you and I can't cope with it.

With a heavy heart, dashed dreams, and a small backpack of belongings, I left, not knowing if I would ever return or if things would ever be the same if I did. It was a lot to bear upon my heart, especially leaving Akash. It felt like leaving half of myself.

He was my best friend for a year. We saw each other daily. We went on countless adventures. We made expeditions out of a walk through the banana fields or a trip to the local markets. Everything was easy and fun with him. Everything felt safe and golden with him.

How could I live without him nearby? Who would come to have chai with me? Who would climb a boulder mountain to watch the sunset with me?

Who would make me laugh when I feel sad? I hate saying goodbye, and I hate it even more when it's someone I want to be beside for the rest of time.

The journey back to New Hampshire was intense. Booking a last-minute flight left very few options. I had to change planes three times, and altogether, including layovers, it took thirty-eight hours to reach my destination. The layovers were long, but I had to get back right away.

Returning to the north in December wasn't ideal. The only clothes I had were summer ones, lightweight and not suited for the New Hampshire winter.

The flights, layovers, lines, and airport chaos were all a blur. The only thing occupying my mind was Jenna and that email:

> *I have a problem, and I need help.*
> *I have an addiction, and I'm really scared.*

She must be drinking too much. What else could it be? Is she taking pills? I used to take muscle relaxers to quiet my mind and rest my body. I sometimes even took them before going into work.

They always made me feel relaxed and warm, almost like the sensation you get after soaking in a hot bath for an hour, surrounded by candles and throwback R&B music.

I never had a problem with them, but I sure did love those pills. Maybe she's taking them and mixing them with alcohol. I also used to love getting drunk and going dancing at nightclubs. I built up quite an alcohol tolerance and was known to go shot for shot with people at the bar.

I never got into trouble with it, though. I stopped when I realized I was getting out of hand. Twelve mixed drinks were excessive and not a path worth continuing. It wasn't difficult to stop. I just decided and did it.

I may have also done a few lines of cocaine on the weekends. It was always social, with other people or sometimes to clean the house or pre-game before a nightclub outing.

I never even tasted good cocaine, so it was easy to turn it down when I wasn't interested anymore. I never felt too attached to it anyway. It was casual, and the high was always short.

Jenna and her dramatic ways. What type of things is

she getting into? I wonder if she got caught driving drunk. That might be enough to scare her.

We'll sort it out as quickly as possible, and then I can go back to Hampi. I'll run back, and everything will return to how it was before I left. I'll live out the rest of my life in bliss and love.

Upon arriving in New Hampshire, I met up with Mother Mary, and we convened at her house in the countryside. I had been living overseas for several years, so it was a long time since we saw each other in person. I've tried to play nice as I've gotten older. Perhaps I've taken Jenna's pleas more into consideration.

Mother Mary stood five feet; seven inches tall. She had brown hair but had been dying it blonde ever since she was in high school. I've only ever seen her with brown roots so it's hard to imagine her without blonde hair.

She had always been beautiful. Even the photos of her from childhood were charming. She learned to leverage her good looks for attention from an early age.

That has always been her superpower. She can get a man. Keep one, well that's a different story. Yet, who needs to keep one if you can get another one tomorrow?

Her steel blue eyes and small gap between her two front teeth were the cherry that sucked you in. Before you even knew what was happening, you were entangled.

Enough so that you were willing to withstand her turbulent mood swings, violent temper, and physiological manipulation.

Even though Jenna and I grew up abused, the truth is, Mother Mary can no longer physically hurt me.

That power has faded with age. She's still quite keen on verbal abuse and manipulation, though, so letting my guard down is out of the question.

As an adult, I have the power to walk away, which lessens the imbalance and forces Mother Mary to play a little nicer. Yet, the rush of being back after so long overrides our tattered history. Not to mention I'm not here for her. I'm here for Jenna.

There was a part of me that was happy to be back in New Hampshire after being away for so long. The crisp, cold winter air revitalized my throat, chest, and lungs.

There's something to be said for breathing in frosty winter air, especially growing up with it. When you leave and then return, it feels like a welcome-home greeting. I missed the sensation of how it felt entering my body. It makes you feel alive.

Jenna arrived at the house later that evening. Mother Mary and I were on the couch watching TV when she entered. She walked past us and acted normal, almost surprised to see me. Jenna did look a little disheveled, but she always looks like that.

Jenna always looks like she needs to brush her hair, change her clothes, and maybe take a nap. That was normal for her. She sometimes looks scattered.

It was part of the price she paid for being overly agreeable. She was always absorbing the worries and needs of those around her. Neglecting herself and the way she presented to the world. She has always happily chosen to pay this toll.

Jenna was five feet ten inches tall. She had long dark brown hair that was wavy but extremely curly when she was a child. She had dark brown eyes and a gap between her two front teeth like Mother Mary.

She had full lips and a freckle under her right eye. Even though she never thought so, Jenna was pretty. She was alluring in a way that never reflects in a mirror. She almost had this rock star quality about herself that contradicted her extreme insecurities.

I couldn't understand how a person could be both nonchalant and insecure at the same time. It was probably because I've never been able to place when Jenna's acting ended, and her authentic-self began.

Jenna was a fantastic actor. She developed it as a survival technique that played into her people-pleasing. It served her well, but it also swallowed her up.

Since she seemed normal, it left me wondering: what was going on? I'm in New Hampshire in December. I was just in India, happy as I had ever been. Could she be putting on an act to keep Mother Mary from worrying? I assumed that we needed to talk in private.

After all, I had just taken a thirty-eight-hour journey here because she sent a distressing email. She and I were going to talk. I was going to find out what that email was about. I'm not known for my patience, and I can be a little demanding.

After waiting about thirty minutes, I'd had enough. I pulled her into the bathroom to figure out what was really going on. Once in the bathroom, she again tried to play it all off and act normal.

She acted like she never sent that email. Was she gaslighting me? Was she hacked? Did someone send me that email to mess with me? Had I just come all this way for absolutely nothing? I swear to God, that better not be the case. I pressed her further.

"What's going on, Jenna? I was just in India by a river, watching an elephant get bathed. Now I'm in New Hampshire in the middle of winter. Why am I here?" I asked as the edge of my patience shown through.

"What do you mean? What are you talking about?" replied Jenna.

"Your email. What's going on?" I insisted.

"Oh. That. Sorry. Don't worry about that. It was nothing. I was just having a bad day and was stressed," Jenna claimed.

"A bad day? I just spent $1,000 to fly here because of your email. You're going to tell me what's going on right now," I insisted. My heart was racing in my chest. I felt doom was near.

"Please, just leave it alone. It's nothing," Jenna begged.

"Jenna, tell me what's going on. Are you okay? You said you have an addiction. To what? Are you drinking?" I implored.

There was a long pause. At least it felt long to me as I waited in anticipation for resolve, some type of reasoning for my trip back.

I kept my gaze locked on Jenna. She looked nervous. I could almost feel the anxiety in her stomach, as if it were my own.

Jenna glanced at the floor and collected her thoughts. She then lifted her head and looked at me.

"Please don't get mad. Promise me you won't get upset if I tell you," Jenna requested.

"Whatever it is, you can tell me," I responded, softening my body to signal safety to her.

Jenna went over to the closed bathroom door and locked it. My stomach dropped. Why did she lock the door? What was she going to tell me?

Was she going to show me something? What if she's cutting herself? My heart raced as fast as my thoughts, trying to figure out what was about to happen next.

She walked back over to me in her sweatshirt and jeans. Jenna grabbed her right sleeve and slowly pulled it up. Then she did the same with the left sleeve to reveal her bare arms. She had marks all over both arms, bruises, scars, scabs.

It looked like a mix of both old and new wounds. I knew what it was, but I also didn't want to know what it was. Both reality and naivety swayed back and forth in my mind. I gently asked, *"What is this? What happened?"*

"I do heroin. I inject it. I've been doing it for a while. Black tar heroin. Please don't get mad," Jenna explained.

I took a step closer to her to get a better look at her arms. I'd never seen that in real life before, track marks. I felt sick. I felt like I was about to throw up.

My God. Is this really happening? Am I dreaming? I rubbed my eyes and shook my shoulders to check. Nope. Not a dream. This was really happening.

My baby sister, the only person in the world I loved with all my heart, is a junkie? A heroin addict? My sweet baby sister has track marks?! Innocent baby Jenna is tainted? As much as I wanted to burst out in an emotional response, I had to stay calm.

The only way she would confide in me was if I remained neutral. I needed to get as much information out of her as possible while she was being vulnerable.

"How much do you take a day?" I inquired.

"A lot," she murmured, eyes fixed on the floor.

"Who sells it to you?" I asked.

"A guy that I know," she mumbled, shifting her weight in discomfort.

"Who taught you how to do that?" I pressed as my body leaned forward.

"Someone I used to know... Please, Amanda, you can't tell Mother Mary," she blurted.

"Why did you do this, Jenna? Why?" I asked, feeling as though the world was bearing down on me.

She looked back at me in a state of half-frozen shock, almost as though she was in as much disbelief as I was. She couldn't believe she'd just told me her secret, and I couldn't believe she had done such an awful thing.

"Please, you can't tell Mother Mary. Please. I'm begging you," she insisted.

Here she goes again, begging and pleading with me to smile and act as if nothing happened. Well, I didn't do it when we were kids, and I sure as hell wasn't going to start now.

Jenna could pull out the best of her manipulation tactics, but she wasn't going to get out of this. Not this time.

"I am leaving the bathroom. You have two minutes to tell Mother Mary. Either you tell her, or I will. Two minutes, Jenna," I commanded.

"Please. Please. You can't," Jenna begged.

"Two minutes starts now," I warned.

I left the bathroom and rejoined Mother Mary on the couch in front of the TV. I felt nauseous. What the hell just happened? My heart was pounding in my chest, and I could barely see anything. I felt like I was in a haze, a fog.

I couldn't hear anything either. The TV had faded so far into the background that I almost didn't hear it at all. A buzz in my head and whirling thoughts were all that existed of me at that moment.

Jenna walked into the living room and stood beside the couch, almost as if she was considering sprinting out of the house at any moment. Two minutes passed, and I gave her a warning. I glanced up at Jenna and pushed, *"Say it."*

"Please, Amanda," she begged as her face contorted in distress.

"Your time is up. Say it, or I will," I demanded, unfazed by her acting.

"Why are you doing this? Please. I can't," she griped.

This doesn't seem to be going anywhere, and I was so sick and tired of her. The manipulation. The begging. The lies. The secrets.

I had been forced to keep many secrets as a child, and maybe that's why I had such a disdain for liars as an adult. I could sniff them out and make their weaknesses known.

I prided myself on my honesty. I don't hold onto secrets, especially those that may eat away at my soul. Jenna had always gotten away with everything. She was the golden child who could do no wrong. But her status was about to be threatened.

I looked over at Mother Mary and asked, *"When was the last time you saw your daughter's arms?"*

"What do you mean?" Mother Mary asked, eyes locked on the TV.

"Think about the last time you saw her arms. How long has it been?" I pressed.

"I'm not sure. Why?" she casually asked in a disregarding manner.

"You need to go look at your daughter's arms. Right now," I demanded.

"What is she talking about, Jenna?" Mother Mary questioned as she finally shifted her gaze from the TV to Jenna.

"Go over and pull up your daughter's sleeves. Right now. Do it," I insisted.

Mother Mary must have gotten a bad feeling because, after a long pause, she made eye contact with Jenna, again. Getting up from the couch, she reached for Jenna's arm as Jenna pleaded in protest.

Mother Mary had an intense grip. She used to punish us in public by grabbing our bare arms and digging her fingernails into our skin.

If we made a scene about the punishment, she'd dig deeper, leaving marks and blood. Evading that grip was futile. She pulled up Jenna's sleeves one at a time and shrieked in horror.

Mother Mary grew up much worse than we did. She was surrounded by drugs, alcohol, guns, and more. She did a terrible job raising Jenna and me, but she sure did try to keep us away from drugs, alcohol, and smoking.

I've never even seen her drink the equivalent of one beer in my entire life. The one thing she did right was that. How must it feel to do one thing right, only for your child to run to the very thing you kept her away from?

The shriek Mother Mary let out when she realized Jenna's arms had track marks was primal. It was purely animalistic.

I had never heard her make that kind of sound before.

I've heard a lot of devilish things come from her mouth, but never a shriek like that.

It was as if her daughter had just died right in front of her, and she was alerting the world as the sound echoed and moved through the atmosphere.

My ears rang and my heart sank from the roar as I shared in its sentiment. What happened next was a natural response, and one that I expected from Mother Mary. She started to beat Jenna.

When we were children, I often shielded Jenna from the abuse. Mother Mary didn't care who or what she was abusing; she just needed to do it.

Since Jenna is younger, I felt it was my duty to bear the brunt of everything that went on in the house. I could handle more than she could because she had an enhanced level of sensitivity.

Don't get me wrong, there were many times when Jenna implemented her *"golden child"* status. She would blame numerous things on me or twist events to make herself look less guilty.

She'd often get me into trouble for her wrongdoings. I took a lot of beatings because of that too.

However, when Mother Mary was feeling extra cruel and mindlessly beating Jenna, I would always step in without a second thought. This was the first time in my life that I watched Jenna get beaten and didn't jump in to rescue her.

She deserved it. I wanted to join in on the beating. I would have loved to have broken her nose or at least given her a bloody lip. How dare she do something so horrific?

Even though I thought about the pleasure of making Jenna bleed, the beating got a little too intense, so I broke it up. Mother Mary quickly retreated to her bedroom and slammed the door shut.

We could hear her screaming and wailing, throwing things, breaking things. Even though I'm an adult, I still fear Mother Mary and her wrath. It would be damn near suicidal to follow her into that bedroom.

We listened as she unleashed her rage onto the bedroom décor, smashing, grunting, bellowing. Part of me would have liked to join her. If only I could get my head to stop spinning.

My heart felt dense, like it wasn't even in my chest anymore. Can your heart leave your chest? I made eye contact with Jenna as she cried. I felt divided.

I wanted to coddle her like she's always been coddled. However, another part of me wanted her to suffer and feel the pain of her actions.

I looked away and let her cry alone as I sat on the couch in disbelief. Everything was different. I felt it in my bones.

Life had shifted before my very eyes, and it seemed permanent. Jenna's secret had been ripped open, revealing a portal that could never be closed.

Exposing her was difficult but it was necessary. The connection within families sometimes seems irrelevant. Until, that is, their lifestyle shatters your own.

The sounds coming from Mother Mary's room buzzed in the background as I disconnected from reality. The room felt like it was rotating, or as though I was in an alternate dimension.

Perhaps I'm dreaming. Please let this be nothing more than a nightmare. I rubbed my eyes and shook my shoulders to check. Nope. This is not a dream. This is my reality.

After ten or fifteen minutes, Mother Mary regrouped. She came back out to the living room, where Jenna and I were sitting in numbness. She had called Jenna's father, Cain.

"Cain is on his way over. We're going to have a meeting," Mother Mary forewarned, pivoting on her heels and walking back to her room.

CHAPTER FOUR

. .
.

"At first, addiction is maintained by pleasure, but the intensity of the pleasure gradually diminishes, and the addiction is then maintained by the avoidance of pain."
Frank Tallis

J enna inherits many of her personality traits from her father, Cain. We have different fathers, and I never knew mine.

Cain was a desperate stand-in for me, and since Jenna and I are only two years apart, we've never considered that we have different fathers.

Cain is social and thrives on interaction with others. He presents as a man who has everything in order. A swift ten-minute audit would reveal otherwise, though. He's the type that needs to be needed.

He'll subconsciously put you in compromising

positions so that he can come to the rescue. Only for you to owe him ten times over once he comes calling for repayment.

The classic narcissist type who can only function within codependent relationships. It doesn't take him long to convince you that meeting his needs is an honor and a top priority.

He's quite the master at it. Don't let his charm fool you. If circumstances were slightly different, Cain could easily start his own cult. I'm sure of it.

Cain must have been speeding because the normal thirty-minute drive took him less than twenty. He entered the house with urgency and curiosity.

A tall man, standing six feet high, with salt-and-pepper hair and a moderate beer belly that was rightfully earned.

He greeted us quickly, eager to get down to the matter at hand. He seemed antsy and anxious. We gathered at the dining room table under a low-hanging light that cast a dusty yellow glow on us.

Mother Mary, Jenna, Cain, and I all sat with our elbows on the table, leaning forward. Everyone was on edge, and it was obvious.

Cain quickly confessed that he had known about Jenna's addiction for many years. He insisted that he had tried everything to get her help and to get her sober.

He claimed that he even sent her to rehab, but she left within weeks. He stammered on about all the ways he had tried to help her.

It was challenging to stay focused on Cain. My head was trying to comprehend the fact that he knew about Jenna's addiction. It felt like a barrier that my brain couldn't get past.

How long had he known? Why didn't he tell Mother Mary? What exactly is unraveling right now? He stammered on like a person with racing thoughts, left all alone with nothing but the sound of their own echo.

He's the one who taught Jenna how to play the game of life through manipulation, lies, and fake facades. He's quite good at it. Very believable, as he works you with his caramel-brown eyes and long eyelashes.

Cain even added that he tried heroin just to see why Jenna found it so appealing. He's a man of the hippie era and is no stranger to drugs or partying.

The very first time I smoked weed, it was stolen from his personal stash, a large gallon-sized Ziploc bag filled almost to the top with marijuana. I must have been around twelve years old.

He always kept it in his briefcase, and you could smell when he had just replenished. Cain would walk into the house and go directly to his room, leaving a scent trail of fresh weed. You didn't need a dog to know what was in there.

The first sip of alcohol I ever had was Jack Daniel's whiskey, kept in the mini fridge in his bedroom. I must have been about eleven or twelve. My curiosity was piqued, wondering why Cain always loved this brown liquid. I had to try it to find out.

I unscrewed the cap, smelled the contents and shriveled back. Determined to know, I placed the bottle to my lips and took a drink. It was horrible. My entire body heaved in opposition.

I couldn't understand why he drank it so often if it burned your throat. This was long after he and Mother Mary had separated. She could no longer control our exposure to drugs and alcohol after their split.

When I was even younger, I remember finding a white substance in his sock drawer. This was when he and Mother Mary were still together. I was far too young to know what it was, but I later heard it was cocaine.

Mother Mary knew how Cain was, but she happily carted me off to his house on weekends along with Jenna. Her peace was more important than our safety. But then again, whose house was better?

Cain proclaiming that he tried heroin for Jenna's sake was such a strange thing to both say and do. I've never tried heroin, but there's absolutely no way I would try it just to understand what Jenna finds attractive about it.

It sounded more like a guilty confession than anything else. Or perhaps it was part of his manipulation tactic, a way for him to show the lengths to which he has tried to help Jenna. I wasn't buying it, though. Not for a moment. He's full of shit.

When I was about thirteen or fourteen, I walked in on Cain smoking weed with a member of his second family, his stepdaughter. She was only a few years older than me.

It was a room full of her friends, and then Cain, holding a joint. His willing participation in trying heroin was jarring but not shocking. I couldn't help but wonder if he tried it with Jenna.

Cain continued sharing with Mother Mary and me about Jenna and her addiction. He seemed to be releasing all the things he had kept bottled up over the years. The stories and information didn't always connect or seem rational.

He sometimes tried to talk in circles. Could it have been because he was backpedaling, or perhaps he was sporadically remembering new details? More likely, he was trying to confuse Mother Mary and me. An amateur move on his part, for sure.

Mother Mary was trained in manipulation by her own devil-spawn of a mother. Mother Mary, in turn, trained me. There were no amateurs on this side of the table, that was for certain.

Cain was methodical enough to paint himself as an innocent bystander who had only ever tried to stop the problem.

Mother Mary and I allowed him to release anything and everything. She and I are similar in the way we catch a lie by focusing on the smaller details. We then use these details as ammunition to burn down the falsehoods.

We were both leaning toward the center of the table, eyes locked on Cain, occasionally glancing over at Jenna. Both of us laser-focused on eventually tripping Cain up with his own words. We were in hunting mode, dead set on a target.

Once Cain started to slow down and pull back from oversharing, Mother Mary and I came in with the questions. As far as I'm concerned, it was the closest I had ever come to a police interrogation.

There were falsities, and we were going to expose them. Mother Mary and I bounced off each other's questions, poking holes wherever possible. She would ask a question, Cain would respond, and I would counter.

It was a doubles tennis match, and Cain was without a partner. All alone on his side of the court, pretending that he wasn't about to collapse with exhaustion.

Pretending that everything was okay. Smiling and pretending, just like Jenna used to try to get me to do when we were children. Her Daddy taught her well.

How could a father keep such secrets from the mother of his only child? He knew she was actively using heroin in his house for years and never once reached out to Mother Mary. What kind of a man does that?

Only a weak coward would withhold such information from a mother. Only a spineless loser would allow such behavior to continue in his home for years.

I was furious at Cain for not exposing Jenna sooner. We could have helped her when it was more manageable. Now it's all spiraled out of control.

The more the conversation went on, the more I hated Cain. My disdain for him kept building. I could feel it climb up my spine and move through my limbs.

My heart was racing, and the angst rose to my throat. My words grew harsher, forming into daggers.

Jenna sat, looking down, doing her best to put on a convincing show of remorse. It was fake. The only thing she felt remorseful about was ever sending me that email to begin with.

That's what made her house of cards collapse. That's what exposed her long-held secret.

I felt myself getting carried away. The extreme emotional experience of the situation along with my fear for Jenna's life were enveloping. After realizing the intensity of my expression and the harshness of my words, I pulled back.

Cain is clearly happy to keep life-threatening information a secret. If I continued to attack him, he would retreat. Since Jenna lives with Cain, he would isolate himself and Jenna further. As much as I hate this pathetic excuse of a man, I had to remain calm. I had to stay neutral.

I had to be fake so he would communicate with me in the future. Even though he's a liar, I had to pretend to have compassion for him and the situation. Even though I wanted to watch him get waterboarded for keeping this from us, I had to remain calm.

I must admit, while I am nowhere near as volatile as Mother Mary, intense emotions are difficult for me. When I am sad, I express sadness. When I am happy, I express happiness. When I am angry, I express anger.

It takes a great deal of restraint for me to be angry and not show it. In a case like this, Jenna's life is on the line. I would sacrifice anything for her, and this is what I needed to do for her right now.

I needed to befriend an enemy. I needed to smile and pretend everything was okay.

Clearly, whatever Cain tried with Jenna didn't work. He wasn't successful, so we needed a new angle. What was the new angle?

Mother Mary and I are strong-willed women. If we try it your way and it doesn't work, then it's time to do it our way.

There won't be any discussions about that either. There are no alternative options.

I both love and hate this about myself. I know it came from her, and it can be an asset, but the delivery isn't always smooth. If only I could combine Cain and Jenna's skillful manipulation with my intentions, I'd be a superpower.

Ultimately, it feels dirty when I manipulate people or am even a little less authentic. So here we go, Mother Mary and I strong-arming our way into the situation.

Cain needed to remove Jenna from his house immediately. Whatever was going on there, it wasn't discouraging her enough to get help. It hadn't swayed her drug usage.

"I'm not kicking my daughter out of her own house. I just won't do it. Where would she go?" Cain scrutinized.

"She can live here with me. Something is going on in that house Cain and this ends now," Mother Mary proclaimed with an authority in her voice that brought back memories of childhood misery.

"It's her house. I won't tell her to leave. She can stay as long as she likes," Cain countered.

"Do you want her to die? She will die if she stays in your house," Mother Mary argued.

"No, she won't. I can handle it. I've been handling it for years. You never even knew anything was going on,"

Cain defended.

"Cain, things need to change. You clearly can't manage your house if you allow drug use," added Mother Mary.

"She is an adult. She can do what she wants. How are you going to force her to live here with you Mary?" Cain taunted.

Cain looked over at Jenna who was still maintaining her best remorseful act. Her head was bowed down and her eyes were focused on her lap. She was convincing but not to me. I knew she was as authentic as a telemarketer with a foreign accent named John Smith.

Cain asked, *"Where do you want to live, Jenna?"*

"With you," Jenna murmured.

What now, Mary?" Cain pressed, his eyes darting toward Mother Mary.

His attitude struck me as interesting. He almost appeared proud of the exchange, pleased with the fact that Jenna wanted to stay with him and that Mother Mary couldn't do anything about it.

Does he think he just won something? Was this supposed to be a jab at Mother Mary? Some past-due divorce scorn to settle? I felt uneasy with the conversation and his tone in general.

Conversing with Cain is exhausting. His

codependency issues make change difficult, especially with Jenna. He will fight to the death, even if it's at the expense of his only daughter's life.

We weren't making any progress and were all emotionally exhausted. The truth is, Jenna is an adult. She's twenty-five years old, and she can do what she likes. We really can't force her to move in with Mother Mary.

To be fair, Jenna moved out of Mother Mary's house before she turned eighteen. It's an abusive house, and it doesn't surprise me that Jenna doesn't want to return.

When I left, I never went back so I understood her resistance. I'd rather sleep on barbed wire than return to Mother Mary's house.

There just weren't any options for her. If I had a place of my own, Jenna could come live with me. I didn't though.

We were stuck at an impasse as no one was willing to negotiate. The only thing I could be sure of at that moment was that this wasn't going to be resolved tonight.

Cain and Jenna said goodbye to us and left, returning to their house. Watching them leave together infuriated me. Heroin is a big deal. A pretty big damn deal.

Why are they not concerned? Jenna could die at any moment. Why are they okay with continuing to do the same thing they've been doing for years? What am I missing?

Heroin, right? I must be missing something. They act

like it's weed or alcohol, a minor issue that needs addressing but isn't overly urgent. Something's off. It's so off that I feel like I'm the one who's wrong, but I know that I'm not.

Mother Mary and I returned to the interrogation table. We needed to hatch our own plan. It's obvious Cain isn't going to assist us. He's on team, active heroin use.

My own experience with drugs is limited. I used to party in my teens and early twenties. I was limited to anything outside of that.

Back then my favorite was muscle relaxers. I loved those. I never had a decent supply, so I stretched them out and only indulged when I had a good hookup.

I liked how they made me feel. Drinking made me an extrovert who danced for hours on end and blacked out. The next morning, I could hardly remember what happened, I just knew it was fun.

Muscle relaxers, though, made me feel warm and loved. I felt so calm and indifferent that I could smile in the middle of a tornado. I could relate to Jenna in that way, but muscle relaxers were far from heroin.

Luckily, I never had an addiction or problem with anything. I could do a few lines of coke, clean my apartment, and then go out clubbing.

My life never revolved around drugs or alcohol. I used them to have fun or relax, or to escape the demons in my head from childhood. Well, mostly it was to escape those demons.

I was different from Jenna in that harder drugs scared me. I'd known people who tripped on acid or mushrooms and had a bad experience.

My head was so dark that I was certain I'd have a bad trip. The stories sounded like a nightmare, and I wasn't willing to try.

Any party drugs like ecstasy seemed like too much for me. I never even knew anyone who tried meth, crack, or heroin. The thought of intense drugs like that never even entered my mind.

They seemed like dirty drugs. Drugs that leave you with rotting teeth, scabbed skin, and living on the streets. Who wants that?

I'd rather get drunk and dance for six hours than end up with rotting teeth and a scabbed face while begging for change on the corner.

As Mother Mary and I sat at the table, we brainstormed ideas on how to get Jenna help. How do we get her away from Cain? They have an odd relationship, and she never wanders very far from him or that house.

Their codependency is too tightly wound. We had to figure out how to create some distance between the two of them so we could get through to Jenna. We could actually help her.

We sat together, allowing any and all ideas to bounce between us. Nothing was off-limits, and everything was under consideration.

"Let's buy drugs, plant them on her, and call the cops to get her arrested," Mother Mary suggested excitedly.

"What if Cain bails her out?" I responded.

"It doesn't matter. She'll have that case against her," Mother Mary chimed in.

"Okay, that might work. Where do we get the drugs?" I asked.

"Do you know anyone?" she inquired.

"I don't know anyone. Maybe I could ride around and try to find something. How do I know what the going rate is?" I added.

I had been away for a long time and no longer had connections to that world. I wouldn't even know if I was getting ripped off. Perhaps that wouldn't matter. I would just need to make sure I got enough for a solid case against her.

"I have no idea," she said with an intense look that felt like it went right through me.   *"What if I get arrested trying to buy them? Hmm... let me ask a few people first,"* I offered.

"What about having her committed?" Mother Mary questioned.

"What do you mean?" I asked.

"We could report that she's trying to hurt herself, and they'd have to come get her and hold her for seventy-two hours," she replied.

"Will she know it's us?" I wondered.

"I'm not sure how it works. I can ask my friend," she added.

"Should we see if we can get her a bed in a rehab?" I asked.

"How do we get her to go?" Mother Mary questioned.

"An intervention, maybe?" I offered.

"That might work," she said.

Mother Mary and I exchanged ideas for hours. We tried to look at the logistics and probability of each one, probing from all angles to see which were the most viable. Both of us were beyond emotions and tuned into action mode. We were going to take command of the situation from now on.

However, the main issue standing in our way was Cain. We knew that even if we came up with a solid plan, as long as Jenna had Cain enabling her, our efforts would be futile. We needed a plan that created a wedge between them.

It was definitely going to be a battle, but we were both ready and able to fight. We loved Jenna beyond measure and weren't going to step aside while Cain led her into the depths of hell, hand in hand.

CHAPTER FIVE

∴

"All journeys have secret destinations of which the traveler is unaware."
Martin Buber

The cold chill of a New Hampshire winter touched my bones. Winter is at its harshest after you've been away from it for a while.

I had forgotten how ruthless the temperature can be and how taunting the wind is. Three pairs of socks and four shirts aren't cutting it. This cold is unbearable.

How did I ever survive here? More importantly, why did I stay for so long? I guess when all you've known is the cold, that's all you can associate with, and the annual suffering that comes along with it.

The killing of plants, animals, and insects. The harsh storms, black ice, hail, and cold nights as you try to conserve energy to reduce the electricity bill. I had forgotten all about it the moment I moved away. Now, back, it felt as though I never left.

The last few winters before leaving, I had a small space heater. One night, I fell asleep on the sofa with it resting on the cushion next to me.

I awoke to a burning smell, only to find that it had tipped over and was burning the sofa. Winters are dangerous.

The suffering eventually gives way to spring, when it all seems justified. We killed it off so we can experience the rebirth.

While it's a beautiful concept, it's not always the most insightful way to live. What if we don't need to suffer for an annual rebirth?

Leaving New Hampshire was one of the best things I ever did. Coming back, though? That's still unfolding. Jenna and I moved around a bit as children. Mother Mary was married to Cain for five or six years before they divorced.

I don't ever remember exactly when they got married, but I do remember they both started wearing wedding rings one day. Even though we relocated several times, we always remained in New Hampshire.

I do have some fond memories of Jenna and me playing in the snow. Mother Mary would force us to play outside, locking the door so we couldn't get back in.

Jenna and I would occupy ourselves with snowmen, snowball fights, snow angels, ice skating, and even a few igloo attempts.

Winter is fun if you're a child, eagerly rushing to the window in the morning to see if there's been a storm, then quickly sprinting to the TV to tune into the local station to see whether school was delayed or canceled.

The best was when school was delayed by two hours, only to find out an hour later that it was canceled altogether.

For some reason, this winter feels colder. Maybe because I've been away for so long and came straight from sultry South India. Maybe it's because life feels like it has changed forever.

The following few weeks were a haze. It was a battle communicating with Jenna and Cain. She would agree to rehab and then disappear or turn off her phone.

Cain was equally elusive or overly vague. The resistance was frustrating. Why was I fighting for Jenna's life when she didn't even seem to care about it?

What superior power do I have over the life of another? Then again, this was my sister, the only sibling I had.

The only person in the entire world that I truly loved. The only person in the world who fully understood me. Jenna was an extension of me. I had to fight for her.

Jenna and I come from the same place. She

understands my brokenness even more than I understand hers. She's never judged me for being broken. She's never made me feel guilty for the parts of me that are missing, shattered, or duct-taped.

When you grow up feeling isolated from the world, having one familiar person who loves you is immeasurable. They become a lifeline to normalcy and security. They make you feel sane in the midst of madness. She was my anchor.

Perhaps Jenna is too beaten down by heroin to care about her own life right now. It's my duty to step in and shield her until she is strong enough to stand up on her own again.

She emailed me asking for help, and I want to fulfill that for her. Yet, why is she redacting her plea? Why is she avoiding my efforts to help?

I couldn't help but wonder about the chances of success under such circumstances. How do you help someone who wants it but then doesn't?

Even if I fight, what am I fighting for exactly? For Jenna to see her own worth? I desperately want to shake her. Grab hold of her and knock her unconscious if necessary.

Whatever it takes to get through, that's what I want to do. I can't figure it out exactly, but it seems as though a spell has been cast upon her, almost as though she's being controlled by a separate entity.

Trying to help her has been frustrating to say the least,

frustrating and confusing. I had no experience with heroin or addiction. I had no idea what to do.

Mother Mary and I decided not to plant drugs on Jenna or have her committed. We wanted to save those options for later. The only thing we kept trying to do was convince Jenna to check into a rehabilitation center.

Cain continued to be of no assistance to us. He only hindered us. He aided and abetted Jenna in her continued drug use. No matter what boundaries we set for Jenna, she had Cain to supply her with everything she needed.

Why would she care if we withdrew resources or relationships from her? Cain was swift to swoop in and make sure Jenna was there to play along in their dysfunctional, codependent relationship.

As long as I'm here battling for her, my own life is up in the air. Obviously, I can't go back to India, at least, not yet anyway. So far, I've made no progress in helping Jenna. If something were to happen, forty hours to return is just too much time.

I need to be close enough to come if there's an emergency, but I don't want to be in New Hampshire any longer. There's too much turmoil for me here.

The history is too complicated and disordered. I don't want to get lured back into anything while I am on a mission to rescue my sweet, innocent baby Jenna.

The decision to leave New Hampshire weighed heavily on my heart. I wanted to leave, but I also needed to be there for Jenna. I couldn't help but feel like a disappointment as well as a bad sister.

I remember how Jenna used to comfort me when we were children. We always shared a room, and when Mother Mary was particularly cruel, Jenna became a source of refuge at night. We would crawl into bed together and take turns crying while the other comforted.

There were many nights when I cried to Jenna, and she would rub my back or play with my hair. She would tell me it was alright, that it was all over, or that tomorrow would be better. She was always there for me.

Childhood left us shattered, but it didn't matter because Jenna always embraced me. She got me through childhood. Without her, I wouldn't be alive.

She never judged or turned away. No matter what, she had always been beside me. There were many people who turned away from me once they saw my brokenness.

It's devastating to be rejected for that. I could, however, always count on Jenna to be there. Her reaching out for help was my opportunity to pay that back. Even just a small amount.

I knew that I needed to leave New Hampshire, even if it felt as though I was turning away from her in ways that she had never done to me. As though I was abandoning her in her time of need.

When I was fourteen years old, I was about to jump off the balcony of our apartment. I was deeply depressed and wanted to end the suffering. I stood on the edge of the balcony, trying to decide whether I should try to land face up or face down.

It was only three stories high, and I wanted to increase the odds of my death. As I contemplated this, I heard a small voice from inside the house.

"Amanda?" Jenna softly called out, with a worried tone.

She knew what I wanted to do. What I was close to doing. The moment I heard her voice; I snapped out of it. I never thought about Jenna. I never thought about what would happen to her if I died or if she would have been the one to find me.

I felt awful for never considering her. The truth is, I was far too consumed with pain to consider anyone or anything else. Jenna saved me that day.

Right now, with her addiction, don't I owe her more than leaving? The truth is, I can't seem to get through to her right now. She is stepping back every time I step forward. Sometimes sprinting back.

I felt frustrated, and regrouping was probably the best

option. Perhaps if I get my own place, she can try to come live with me. Then I might have an opportunity to get through to her. I had to get myself in a better position to leverage more concise assistance.

I packed up the Toyota I had stored while I was overseas. Every possession I owned fit into the trunk. I like living this way, to be honest. It's freeing.

I can pack up all my belongings in under thirty minutes and fade off into the distance. It reminds me of the song "Free Bird" by Tom Petty, just a bird setting off into the sunset.

Part of me feels like a horrible sister, but the other part is being logical. I obviously can't do anything here.

Or whatever I have been doing for Jenna isn't working. Switching up the strategy increases the odds. I desperately needed to increase the odds.

It was necessary for me to find a place of my own to live. I needed to take care of myself to take care of her. I had no destination in mind.

The only goal was to migrate away from the harsh winter but stay close enough to return quickly if something were to happen.

Since I hadn't had any source of income for over a year, my funds were limited. This meant that I would be sleeping in the car until I could figure out my next step.

Luckily, traveling had increased my tolerance for rough accommodations. I can fall asleep in uncomfortable places and surroundings.

I can't tell you how many times I've fallen asleep at a bus station, at a table in a rest stop, or on death-defying bus trips through the mountains of Nepal. I've even been known to fall asleep in the middle of a party or two.

Unsurprisingly, even as a child, I had always been great at sleeping. I love to sleep, it's serious business. I can't stand feeling tired, that tingling sensation in my eyes and mental disconnect.

Even fighting to keep my eyes open. It's so uncomfortable. I know most people suck it up and grab a coffee, but I bow out and find a patch of grass to rest.

As a child, Mother Mary hated waking me up. She would get so frustrated that she began throwing water on me in the mornings.

For some reason, she wouldn't allow me to use an alarm clock. She had heard it was bad for your heart, so she took mine away and insisted on waking me up herself.

The problem was that she hated waking me up and would get aggressive about it. I never wanted to get up, and Mother Mary never wanted me to stay asleep.

It was not the best way to start the day. I could never make much sense of that, even now. Her forcing me to surrender my alarm clock so she could get frustrated and angry. Perhaps it was just another fun way for her to torment me. Who knows?

I was packed and ready to leave New Hampshire. I said my goodbyes to Mother Mary, but Jenna was MIA. It didn't exactly surprise me. I have to admit, I was still slightly disappointed.

She was my sister, and we were supposed to be close. I forced myself to diminish those feelings and rationalize that it was fine.

I, myself, hated saying goodbye and had left many people in Hampi without sharing a few final words. Perhaps Jenna is similar. When it hurts too much to bear, it's easier to evade it. I'll reconnect with her once I get settled somewhere.

Driving over the border and into Massachusetts brought a heaviness to my heart. Unsure if I was doing the right thing, I could only hope for the best.

With no real direction or destination, I wandered the highways for several weeks. Where do you go when you have no place to go? Having too many options is my problem. I guess it's a decent problem to have.

I made a few stops along the journey as I traveled south. I reconnected with some old friends. Having been gone for these past few years felt like a time warp. My life had been fun and adventurous. I felt as young as I did when I left.

Coming back and visiting old friends made me realize that time did, in fact, pass while I was away. People got married, had babies, started businesses, relocated, and even died.

Time moves whether you like it or not. Whether you're ready for it or not. Whether you want it to or not.

Even though I was happy with my escapades and exotic stories, I couldn't help but feel like everyone was ahead of me in life. They had more established existences with responsibilities and commitments. Here I was, rolling up with everything I owned in the trunk of my Toyota and a small amount of money in the bank.

They all seemed like official adults, shuffling off to work, eating a packed lunch, enduring rush hour traffic on the way home, playing with their children, going to bed, and waking up to do it all over again.

When did that happen? How did I miss the roll call to become an adult? Would they come back around for me?

I was excited to see everyone again and happy to share my adventures. However, it was clear that we were all different now. Life was different.

I thought meeting up with old friends would bring me some comfort during these unsettling days. However, it left me feeling a deeper sense of isolation.

They could no longer relate to me, nor could I with

them. I went from being a partying college student straight to traveling the world.

Now, here I was, circling back around, only to find out that while I was in far-off lands, they were becoming obliging members of society. They had all established roots.

Feeling the massive disconnect from my old friends and acquaintances, I guess it was just me and my Toyota for the time being, prowling the highways and flying in the wind. Not having a direction is sometimes freeing, but sometimes it's frustrating.

I had thoughts of going out west, so I began traveling in that direction. Then I also thought about going to Florida. Only old people live in Florida, though, so what would I do down there? Before I knew it, I was in Nashville.

The truth is, I crashed my car thirty minutes outside of Nashville. While making a left-hand turn, I forgot to double-check traffic and pulled out in front of an older model SUV. My airbags deployed, and the Toyota was totaled.

During the crash, I slammed my left forearm against the steering wheel, and the pain was tremendous. I got out of the car and just stood there in shock and disbelief.

That Toyota was all I had. Everything I owned was in the trunk. I had no place to go and hardly any money in the bank. My arm hurt and bruised almost instantly. I was stunned and went numb. I was too distressed to cry.

The police arrived at the scene and took statements from both me and the other woman involved. Coming from New Hampshire, car insurance was optional if your car was paid off, and my car was.

This meant I had no insurance. Being in the state of Tennessee during the accident, the other driver was required to have car insurance, but she did not.

This meant the accident was declared *"no fault,"* and neither of us was guilty. The other driver got a ticket for her lack of insurance. Even though her SUV was damaged, she was able to drive away.

I was left with the police officer and the tow truck as they loaded my prized possession onto the flatbed. My heart was racing. Was I going to have to sleep on the streets tonight?

I told the officer that I had relocated and that everything I owned was in that car. I asked him if he thought a local trucker might take me into Nashville.

He advised me not to, but I had no other options at that point. The officer could sense my distress and offered to drive me into Nashville and drop me off at the Greyhound bus station. I happily accepted the ride and was relieved to get into his warm car.

My arm became increasingly more painful, but I was trying to ignore it. The officer was gracious and kind, and we chatted the entire drive into the city. He dropped me off at the Greyhound station and advised me to get a bus ticket back home.

That's an interesting word, *"home"*. What do you do if you don't have one? Sometimes it feels like it's everyone's favorite word. For those of us without a home, the word feels like a painful reminder of what we lack in life.

The evening darkness had settled by the time we arrived. It must have been after 9 PM, and the bus station was a seedy place.

Since there is no home, there is no ticket there. I waited until the officer's car was out of sight before walking away from the bus station.

I had no idea which direction to walk or where I was going. It was late at night. I was all alone. It was my first time in Nashville, and my arm was in agonizing pain.

The first priority was finding a place to sleep. If I was going to sleep outside, I didn't want it to be in this area of town.

Long-distance bus stations are always in the grimiest places, even in other countries. It's as though they intentionally plan to put these types of bus stops in the worst areas of town.

Even though my heart was racing, I had to find a place to sleep. After walking for about ten minutes, I noticed a city bus stop where some people were waiting. That must mean a bus was due to arrive soon. I joined the others in waiting for the city bus.

It wasn't long before one came along and stopped. After boarding the bus, I realized I had no change or cards to pay. I told the driver the story of my accident in hopes that he would let me ride for free, and that he might know of a safer area for me.

The man was kind and empathetic as he reassured me that everything would be okay. Luckily enough, there were several motels on his route. Weight lifted off my chest and I could have kissed the man's feet in salvation.

Before long the bus driver dropped me off at the entrance of a motel. I was beyond grateful as he handed me $40 in cash. What a blessing.

I thanked him as a tear dropped down my cheek. Hurrying off the bus, I ran into the reception room of the motel.

There was a room available, and the employee accepted my $40 as payment for the night. I hurriedly made my way to the room and locked the door behind me. A sigh of relief left my body as the sound from the deadbolt signaled safety.

The pain from my arm was getting more intense. I ran a bath with hot water and placed my forearm in it. The warmth slightly eased the discomfort, but it was only momentary. I've never hurt my arm like that before. Maybe it's sprained.

I couldn't stop myself from thinking that everything was falling apart as I paced in the room. My mind went numb in an attempt to shield myself from an emotional breakdown. This was undeniably bad and I was afraid.

CHAPTER SIX

∴

"We don't meet people by accident. They are meant to cross our path for a reason."
Unknown

On the bus ride over, I noticed a Waffle House across from the motel. Even though it was late at night, a thought popped into my head, *go have a coffee.*

I'm not sure where the thought came from because I'm not a coffee drinker and leaving the motel room was the last thing I wanted to do.

Nonetheless, I needed to do something to take my mind off the accident, my arm, and the future. I made my way across the street to the Waffle House. I sat at the counter, ordered water, and let my thoughts swirl.

With my head resting on the counter, I tried to figure out what to do the next morning. I didn't even have a change of clothes. Where would I go? I could pay for a few more nights at the motel, but what then?

I didn't have enough money to buy a car, and I didn't even know where I was headed. All my possessions were in the Toyota, how would I even get them? My arm throbbed, and I wanted to cry, but I was too petrified. The tears just wouldn't come.

A few seats down from me, two older men in their seventies must have sensed my distress. One of them came over, sat beside me, and asked if I was alright.

That simple question opened the floodgates. I began to cry and boy, did I cry. It all came rushing out. Jenna's addiction, the car crash, the police officer, the bus driver, my arm.

They sat and listened, offering comfort, napkins, and even a cup of coffee. Being vulnerable is something I'm not accustomed to, let alone being vulnerable with complete strangers. But it felt good to let it all out, to share my troubles with others.

Sometimes, we carry more than we realize. I do this more than I'd like to admit, holding onto pain and regret until it becomes so familiar that I no longer notice the weight. The two men, Isaac and Jacob, listened patiently and waited until I calmed down.

Once I was relaxed enough to compose myself, they

wasted no time as they promptly began resolving my dilemma. They offered to meet me in the morning to help with the logistics of getting my car and belongings. That alone made me feel better.

Jacob, a Waffle House regular, claimed to know the manager and promised me a job as a waitress. That way, I could find a place to stay and save enough money to continue my journey.

He even called over a waitress and had her bring me a job application. I graciously accepted the offer and the help they extended.

I figured that it was highly improbable that they would follow through with their offers of assistance. The words and plans alone relieved the pressure I felt from the situation.

It gave me hope that no matter what, it would be okay. Car or not. Belongings or not. Motel or not. I would survive.

After I had my fill of coffee and crying, I said goodnight and returned to the motel. I never expected to see Isaac or Jacob again, but I was exhausted and just needed sleep. I would have to figure things out tomorrow.

When I woke up, the pain in my arm was excruciating. How long does a sprain take to heal? Through the window, I could see the sun penetrating past the curtains. It was time to face the day. I wished I were still asleep, in a dream.

I got myself together as best as I could and headed

down to the reception area to check out. To my amazement, Isaac was there. He was casually chatting with the employee, smiling as they exchanged pleasantries.

I approached him, a huge smile on my face. I couldn't believe it, he showed up. I felt like a child on Christmas morning. Overjoyed. Loved.

He had promised to help me retrieve my things from the tow yard, but I never thought he actually would. And yet, here he was, ready to make good on his word.

Isaac smiled back and said in his thick southern accent, *"You ready? Let's go get your stuff."*

Isaac escorted me to his car, opened the passenger door, and waved me in. I slid in with a childlike eagerness. He walked around to the driver's side, got in, and we drove to the tow yard. Isaac offered to store my items until I could figure out my next move.

I was uncertain about the arrangement since I didn't know him, but what other options did I have? I was being charged daily for storing my car, and I couldn't access my belongings.

I had to trust Isaac, blindly. What if he took off with my possessions? What if he sold them or pretended he never met me? These were all risks I had to take.

After some encouragement from Isaac, I sold my car to the tow guy. I signed away the title and received $250.

This was a Toyota Corolla with under sixty thousand miles, fully paid off. I couldn't help but feel a pang of regret. All the overtime I worked to pay that car off.

I had worked at a factory when I bought the car. For two months, I worked overtime, seven days a week, with shifts lasting twelve hours.

I was proud of myself when I signed the papers for it. It was the first brand-new car I had ever bought, with just thirty miles on it when they handed me the keys.

I continued to work overtime to pay off the loan early, regularly making extra payments. A seven-year loan was paid off in just four. It was my biggest purchase to date and paying it off early was a day I celebrated.

It symbolized my effort to better my life, proof that I could achieve something despite my torturous childhood.

When I left to go overseas, I knew I had to keep the car. I stored it, unsure when or if I would return. It represented my determination and dedication.

But now, I was reduced to $250 for all that effort, work, and perseverance. It felt like it had been for nothing. Standing in the cold, hard office of the tow yard, I was defeated.

To others, it was just a car, a physical possession that could easily be replaced. But to me, it was a symbol that I could achieve anything if I worked hard enough. It represented the possibility of a better life, a life I deserved after everything I had been through.

After getting the cash, Isaac helped me transfer my belongings from the Toyota to his. I felt a twinge of sadness and tried to hide the tears streaming down my face. I swallowed hard, forcing the lump in my throat to go away.

I hated always having to be strong. Why couldn't I be one of those women who have an easy life? A calm, relaxed and secure life.

Isaac and I returned to his car, and we started our drive back to Nashville. He kept the conversation light, reminding me that it was just a car and that life moves on.

"There are plenty of cars in the world, honey. Once you get a little money saved, you can get any one you want," he offered.

He was right. It's just a car. I couldn't help that I still wanted to cry though.

"Don't you worry for nothin'," he reassured, eyes glancing in my direction.

Isaac meant well, but my heart wasn't in it. All I could think about was the hard work that went into paying off my Toyota. My one and only asset, gone. I was now stranded.

Even though I was upset, the accident had been my fault. I hadn't taken the extra glance when making a left turn, and I didn't have insurance. My actions put me in that position, but it didn't make it hurt any less.

As we neared the city, Isaac told me he had paid for the motel for the next four nights so I could get on my feet and find a job. I couldn't believe it.

Did this stranger really just pay for my stay? As Isaac dropped me off at the motel, he made sure my spirits were lifted.

"Now listen here. You're gonna go get you that job at Waffle House. All you do is bring 'em the application and I'll see to the rest," he declared.

As I began to walk away, he yelled, *"Don't you go sit in that room and cry neither. Go make some friends."*

Some people's kindness is overwhelming, it knocks you off your feet. My heart swelled with gratitude for this incredible act of generosity. I couldn't thank him enough. He would never truly understand the depth of my admiration because words could never be enough.

For the next few days, I was on a mission to get a job and figure out where to live. I needed money, so staying in Nashville for a short time made sense.

That way, I could buy a car and keep moving toward my unknown destination. I filled out the Waffle House application and started working the very next day.

Being a waitress at Waffle House was intimidating. The clientele was tough, and the tips were small. I even had to learn how to call out orders to the cooks.

It felt like the entire restaurant was looking at me as I awkwardly did my best. Sometimes, it was hard to believe this was where I was, but I was grateful it was only temporary.

The final year that I lived in Australia, I was a waitress. People were more laid-back in Australia, to say the least. I had interviewed for a job at a beachside restaurant near Perth, intending to be a food runner or a hostess.

They hired me on the spot and told me I'd be waitressing that same night. I like to pretend I'm relaxed, but in reality, anxiety is always simmering under the surface. When they told me, I was starting that night, my skin felt like it was peeling off.

When I returned later that day for my first shift, I was given no training, none at all. The manager simply handed me a paper and pen and said, *"Take that table's order."*

He pointed to a couple sitting in the corner. I forced one of the other waitresses to come with me for support as she laughed at my fear. As with everything I worry about, it turned out fine.

What I loved about that restaurant was the view. The entire dining room overlooked the beach, with tall glass windows that spanned the entire length of the building.

There was also an outdoor patio area. The building

was literally on the beach, and the staff would often go for a swim in the ocean during breaks.

My favorite shift was the evening one, though. That's when I could watch the sunset over the ocean and stroll the empty beach at night after I got off work.

It was peaceful and calming. I love the beach at night, it's always deserted, the sand is cool, the sound of the waves seems louder, and you can gaze at the stars while inhaling the fresh, salty air. Visiting the beach at night is severely underrated.

Nonetheless, Waffle House was the opposite of that. There, we had to memorize the menu, learn a code for calling out orders, bus tables, wash dishes, clean the restrooms, and hustle for a $1 tip. Some shifts, I'd leave with $20. Maybe $60 on a good day.

The work was intense, and the people were just too rough for me. You can't have thin skin and work here. They will eat you alive. I'd been yelled at, propositioned, disrespected, and left without a tip, among many other things.

I never worked the night shift because there had been gunfights, and I wasn't interested in dying for that $1 tip. The manager wasn't the nicest person either. I assume she had been toughened by Waffle House as nothing was ever good enough or fast enough for her.

Even though she was stern, I was promised a

management position after a three-month probationary period. Unfortunately, after five months and several inquiries, I realized it was a ploy. What was a college-educated person doing at a Waffle House, anyway?

Luckily for me, I found an apartment to rent within the first week of being in Nashville. It was an African lady looking to rent out the second bedroom in her apartment. She seemed nice when I met her, and I moved in right away with a three-month agreement.

The room was unfurnished and had no ceiling light. So, after a long shift, I'd go back home and lay on the floor. I kept my bedroom door open so I could use the hallway light to see.

I hated sleeping on the floor because it always made my hips and back feel weird. However, I had a place to stay, so I wasn't too worried about it.

Plus, my lease was only for three months. I hoped to be ready to move on by then, so there was no sense in buying any furniture.

To be completely honest, I really missed India. I cried regularly for the village. Life was drastically different now and I felt alone. I often called Akash to check in with everyone. God, I missed him.

While in Hampi, I made great friends with a young sixteen-year-old girl who ran her family's fruit cart. Her name was Roshni. We met the first week I arrived. She sold a variety of fruits that her mother bought from a few towns over.

The village is somewhat of a tourist destination, so they could charge a premium to foreigners. I already knew the local prices for most things in India, so when she tried to scam me on our first meeting, I called her out and got a better deal on some fruits. From that moment on, we became friends, and I visited her regularly.

Roshni was the middle child, with both an older and a younger sister. Her older sister was married with three children of her own, and her younger sister was in school. Roshni was left to support her family as best she could.

I loved visiting her during the day. We always had great laughs, especially when tourists would come to buy fruit from her, and she would wildly mark up the price.

We'd giggle about it as they walked off with their bunch of bananas or ripe mangoes. I was on her side and wanted her to make money for her family.

Since Roshni was always selling fruit, we never really got to go on adventures together. Our escapades always took place at the fruit cart.

I missed her desperately. I missed our laughs and how we talked about life and the future. She's the one who taught me that God, or your concept of it, resides within your heart.

I arranged to have money sent to her and her family

with the help of Akash. Such a small amount of money for me was a huge amount for them. I loved many people in Hampi.

My heart ached for them regularly. My heart also ached for India in general. I missed the lifestyle.

So much, in fact, that I had reverse culture shock, and life in the US seemed intense and isolating. In India, I was never alone.

There was always a villager to talk to, a child to play with, or a person to sip chai with. In the US, I was alone and reminded of that regularly.

Even going to the grocery store seemed overwhelming. An entire aisle of bread. An entire aisle of cereal. An entire wall of yogurt. In India, you have one to three options.

In the US, you have endless options. Regardless of the variety, the meaning of life is different. There's an emptiness that I can't ignore. Or perhaps the emptiness was just me.

I couldn't hide how difficult it was being back in the US. I absolutely hated every moment of it. I felt as though I left my heart and soul in India, and I was trying to survive without them. I can't go back, though, because of Jenna. I was only here for her.

I just hoped I would return to India sooner rather than later. I hoped they would all remember me once I did go back. Would everything sink back to how it was before I left?

I fantasized about the village and my return. Especially at night as I drifted off to sleep. I could visit them each night.

Perhaps I only felt this way because my life was too different now. It was rough, cold and undesirable. I was sacrificing what I desperately wanted to help Jenna. Maybe I was a little more than bitter about that.

CHAPTER SEVEN

.·.

"You cannot wish for both a strong character and an easy life. The price of each is the other."

John Ortberg

After working at Waffle House for two weeks, I came to a conclusion. Well, Isaac and Jacob forced me into it.

They would regularly visit me during my shifts to say hello and sit in my section so they could tip me well.

My forearm just wasn't getting any better. I had kept it wrapped in an Ace bandage and wore a long-sleeve shirt to hide the injury. I really needed the waitressing job, and I didn't want them to know I was hurt.

However, Jacob forced me to go to the hospital to get it checked out. I didn't have health insurance, so I was reluctant to get it looked at. He encouraged me to go by informing me that there was a program at the hospital that would fix it for free.

That very same week, I followed his instructions and got it checked. Turns out that sprain was actually a broken forearm. That's right, I had a broken arm for two weeks and was waitressing.

The doctor said it was already starting to fuse back together and that there would always be a bump because of that. I was slightly upset at having a bump but thought it might make for an interesting "war story" to tell one day: the time I broke my arm, and it took me two weeks to get it checked out.

At the end of my first appointment, the doctor tried to force me to accept a prescription for pain medication. Even after politely declining several times, he still tried to pressure me into accepting the prescription scribbled onto a piece of paper.

I had to get boisterous and cause a scene for him to leave me alone. Why would I need pain medication if I had been walking around with a broken arm for two weeks already? I was quite sure the worst was already over.

The instant any professional tries to force medication onto me is the very moment I lose all respect for them. He had no idea what my history was. I could have been a recovering addict for all he knew.

Especially with everything going on with Jenna, I was

hypersensitive to the fixation doctors have on medications.

I've had several bad experiences with doctors, including some who have tried to force me to take medication. They will go as far as to say, *"Just accept the prescription and save it for later,"* or *"Save it just in case you ever need it."*

I even had one who suggested that someone I know might need the prescription. It's atrocious behavior to say the least.

This doctor fixing my arm is nothing more than another addition to the running list. That's probably why I never like going to doctors. They supposedly took an ethical oath but never uphold it.

The entire opioid epidemic started because of doctors and the kickbacks they received from prescribing them. I can't help but question how genuine their care is.

I was eventually fitted with a cast and sent on my way. I was happy to leave his office and even happier to start healing my arm. The doctor suggested I take a few supplements to aid the healing, so I grabbed them before heading back home.

This was the first time I had ever broken a bone. I always thought bone had to be poking out of your skin for it to be broken. Now I definitely know better.

I continued to hide the injury at work because I didn't want to risk getting my hours cut. It was challenging to keep up with demand using only one arm. Carrying loads of dishes to the sink and washing them was particularly difficult.

Though, with the cast, I no longer felt sharp, shooting pain when I did so. There were several times at work when the pain took my breath away as I hurried to the restroom to cry.

I made Isaac and Jacob promise not to tell my manager about the injury. As usual, they kept their word.

Everything at the apartment was going well. The African lady, Rachel, was quiet, and we stayed out of each other's way. About one month into living there, Rachel asked if a woman from her church could move in and stay in the living room. I was fine with it, as long as all bills and rent were split into thirds.

Delilah moved into the living room and seemed fine. She came across as a friend, but I later realized she was actually just digging for dirt.

She was the type who liked to gossip and spread rumors. Both women were highly active in the church which made Delilah's tendencies more entertaining than anything else.

I have never been religious. I always thought that if there was a God, He was evil and cold. How else could I explain my childhood abuse? If there was a God, was He watching me, as a child, get kicked while in the fetal position?

Was He listening when Mother Mary drilled into my

head how stupid, useless, ugly, and worthless I was? Did He witness me cry as I contemplated taking my own life because the pain was unbearable?

What kind of God allows children to be abused? What kind of God allows children to be neglected, unloved, and rejected? Not any kind that I want to praise, that's for sure.

As humans, we search for answers and meaning to almost everything. If we can't find it, we create it. I struggled to find meaning in my childhood. How do you assign meaning to abuse? What could possibly be the purpose of it?

The only concept of God that I had was that there was something greater to me. There was more to life than suffering.

I did see the synchronicities to the Universe as a whole, the coincidences that couldn't truly be accidental. Anything more than that was unknown, and I had no desire to know.

I suppose I'm slightly tainted when it comes to religion. Mother Mary took us to church for a few months while growing up.

We didn't want to go but she forced us. We never discussed religion or God and then one day she decided that we were going to be religious.

Sitting on the stiff church pew I looked up at her. The woman who tormented me daily, dressed in her best, intently listening to the lecture on God and goodness. I hated her.

Perhaps that angst partially transferred to God. Rachel and Delilah reminded me of that animosity. I could have been projecting those sentiments onto them. Maybe they weren't two-faced like Mother Mary.

Even though the two-bedroom apartment now had three women in it, we seemed to make it work. I preferred to stay away as much as possible and avoid the kitchen, too. The less we interacted, the less there would be a chance for conflict.

My expenses were low now that we split everything into thirds. I wanted to ride this arrangement out until the very end. Rachel and Delilah hosted a Bible study group on Wednesday evenings.

It just so happened to be the exact time I was at the gym. This was not one of those universal coincidences. Call it accidental if you like, but it very much was intentional.

One afternoon at the Waffle House, Isaac asked how it was going at my new apartment. I told him it was good, but that I needed to buy a mattress because I had been sleeping on the floor.

His jaw nearly dislocated as he looked at me in horror. *"You don't have a bed?"* he said in a drawn-out southern accent.

"Not yet," I replied.

"Well, what have you been sleepin' on, honey?" he inquired.

"A blanket on the floor," I responded.

"Well, we're just gonna to have to do something about that today, now aren't we?" Isaac chimed.

"It's fine. Please don't buy me anything. You've already helped me so much," I acknowledged.

"Honey, I'm not gonna buy you nothin'. What I am gonna do, though, is stop by my storage unit and see what I can bring on over to you. Do you need anything else, other than a bed?" he probed.

"Well, there isn't a light in my room, so maybe a lamp or something," I suggested.

"No bed and no light? You just sit alone, on the floor, in the dark after work?" he smirked.

I smiled and remained silent because it's basically true. I had to admit that it did sound rather pathetic when you say it out loud. I was slightly embarrassed by my roughness, yet equally impressed. I really did have some rather low standards.

Call it low maintenance if you like, but sleeping on the floor was the least of my worries. Isaac had the most charming southern way of seeing right through you. You couldn't hide much from that man, and he wasn't shy about putting it into words.

"Will you be home around five or six tonight?" Isaac asked.

"Yes," I responded with a smile and tilted head.

"Well, I'll see you then," he asserted.

In perfect Isaac fashion, he did show up later that evening, just after six o'clock. He had his Astro van jam-packed with stuff.

I couldn't help but feel guilty that a man in his seventies had been moving furniture around for me. I ran outside to meet him and started unloading all the treasures he brought over.

He had two lamps, a bed, a box spring, a bed frame, a dresser, and a chair. It was all older furniture from when Isaac lived in a larger house before his wife had passed away.

He had lots of it in storage, and it had just been sitting there. Here I was, reaping the rewards of all those years this furniture had been waiting in the wings. I was beyond grateful to Isaac.

I suppose this is what it feels like to have a father or maybe a grandfather. I never knew my father, and my grandfather, well, I could count the number of times we've met.

He's always lived on the West Coast while we lived on the East Coast. We usually saw him once a year when he would visit other family members in the Northeast.

We would spend a few hours together and then part ways. He is Mother Mary's father, and she has no relationship with him either. Maybe Jenna and I never had a relationship with him because Mother Mary never did.

If you asked me a question about him, I wouldn't be able to tell you much. Not having a solid male figure in your life changes you.

It makes women harsher and more masculine. It long proved to them that men were unreliable, not to be trusted, or just shadows in the wind.

As for my own father, who knows that story. I used to ask Mother Mary about him, and she would always get angry and aggressive.

After doing that a few times, I learned not to speak his name. Even though I really wanted to know, it wasn't worth a beating later.

We met briefly when I was ten years old. I wondered if it was somehow connected to Mother Mary receiving child support payments. I never knew him and then, one day, he was there.

He took me skiing and bought me a soccer ball. We only met a few times before he was just another figure in the wind.

He disappeared, and I never got any kind of explanation. As a child, I thought I wasn't good enough for him. Perhaps all those nasty words that Mother Mary had drilled into me were true. Perhaps I was nothing. I was meaningless. I was ugly.

Otherwise, why would my father leave me for the second time without ever saying goodbye? A child can't grasp that and as an adult, it's not that much less confusing. It broke my young heart and left a layer of unresolved feelings to envelop me for many years to follow.

With all the new furniture Isaac brought over, I slept better than I had in a very long time. I passed out almost instantly as my body was rewarded with the experience of a mattress.

My back and hips were pleased with the new sleeping situation, and I loved being able to close the bedroom door because now I had light in the room.

I felt spoiled. I felt rich. I felt blessed. I felt loved. Isaac and the southern gentlemen were a blessing. They felt like angels showering me with abundance.

Neither Isaac nor Jacob ever told me much about themselves. They were both retired and enjoying the end of their lives. Isaac was a manager at a large company and Jacob worked for himself. Their children were grown, and both of their wives had passed away.

I wasn't the first troubled woman to blow into Nashville and across their path. I definitely wasn't the last either. They were generous men who were always willing to assist with open arms.

I treasured that about them. Even though they had been taken advantage of, they remained untainted and benevolent.

The three-month apartment lease came and went. Rachel said we could just continue with the same arrangement. However, Delilah kept asking, either directly or indirectly, if I was going to move out.

I'm pretty sure she was tired of being in the living room and wanted to take my room. Who could blame her. She had almost no privacy.

Rachel was the official tenant on the apartment lease, and she used the kitchen at all hours of the day and night. I couldn't imagine trying to sleep in the living room with Rachel banging around pots and pans just a few steps away.

I was fine where I was, though, and had zero intentions of giving up the bedroom or leaving. With rent and utilities split three ways, I was only paying under $500 a month for everything.

I needed my bills to be as low as possible so I could buy a car. The bus was getting kind of tiring because it was often either super late or just early enough for you to miss it.

Luckily, I lived on the same street as the Waffle House, so I only needed to ride it a few miles straight down the road.

The weather was still cold, colder than I expected. I never realized that Nashville got snow and ice and was as frigid as it was.

My feet would always go numb as I waited at the bus stop. Moving around, stomping my feet, never made a difference either.

I hated the winter, and I especially hated waiting for public transport in the cold. I'd always had a car in New Hampshire, so waiting for the bus in the cold was a new experience.

Even though they get snow here, there is almost no winter planning. When a storm rolls through, everything closes until the snow melts. Anyone who lives on a hill or steep incline must wait for everything to thaw.

After one storm in particular, Waffle House paid for all employees to stay at the motel behind the restaurant. They gave me a room for three days with free meals at the restaurant. I could've made it home, but I wanted a few days away from the apartment.

Being from the north, it was shocking that banks were closed because of three to five inches of snow, and that your waitressing job would put you up in a motel for several days and feed you. Northerners would never even believe me if I told them.

I've been in Nashville for several months and I still

don't have enough money saved up for a car yet. The tips are tiny at Waffle House, and I have a very low credit score from being overseas for all those years. I'm feeling slightly pressured to move out of the apartment, but I need to hang on as long as possible.

Jenna and I stayed in contact as much as possible. It wasn't always easy getting a hold of her or getting her to respond to my texts or emails.   When she did come out of hiding, I remained neutral and tried to get her to agree to either go to rehab or come stay with me.

She would mostly evade the topic by changing the subject or getting aggressive in an attempt to intimidate me. Some conversations were better than others. There were a few when she seemed to slightly lean toward the side of wanting to get help.

However, I could tell she wasn't completely genuine about it. Sometimes it seemed like she would say anything just to change the conversation or get me to stop asking.

I was still confused about the entire situation. Why ask me for help if you're just going to refuse it? I still didn't understand. Perhaps it was because I hardly ever ask anyone for help.

I'd rather drown than ask for assistance. I'd be too mortified to ask someone for help, only to turn around and refuse it.

Maybe that's why I couldn't understand. Conversely, it could have just been Jenna seeking attention again. If she asks for help and then refuses it, she almost has you on a hook.

She could control your emotions and have you begging her for basic conversations. It was possible that she felt empowered by that dynamic, perhaps one of the very few situations where she felt like that.

As much as I love her, I cannot relinquish how much I have sacrificed for her. She upended my world, and now I could hardly get her to respond to emails. There was a part of me that hated her. I couldn't deny that this part existed.

My life in India had been a fantasy come true. I obtained things I never really thought could exist for me. I was the happiest I had ever been. My heart was calm and settled.

Now, here I was in the country music capital, Nashville, living with two pretentious church girls, waitressing at Waffle House, without a car, and scraping together everything I had. All for a girl who hasn't made an effort in our relationship for over a decade. I was frustrated.

When I was traveling overseas, I used to email Jenna regularly. I offered for her to join me, with all expenses paid. I dreamed of traveling the world with her, just two sisters exploring countries and making the most epic memories together.

I asked her to come join me in Australia several times. I would pay for everything, including her passport. She could live with me, and we could find her a job. Unfortunately, she always refused the offer.

I asked her to join me in India, with all expenses paid. We could eat curry, ride elephants, and sip chai as we overlooked the sunset.

She refused the offer. I was in Hawaii for six months and invited her to come visit me, all expenses paid. We could buy matching Hawaiian shirts, chase rainbows, and go hiking. She refused the offer.

Anytime I went to a new place or a new country, I would offer her a free trip to come see me. Yet, every single time, she would refuse. I thought she was jealous of me, that I had made it out of our childhood and was thriving.

I had banished the demons that Mother Mary inserted into my head and was living an impossible dream. My life was free and fun.

All I ever wanted was for Jenna to follow me to that freedom, to that fun. I wanted to share how I did it and where the shortcuts were. I wanted to live a happy and healthy life with Jenna by my side.

Each time she declined my travel offers, my heart sank. Each call, text, or email that went unanswered pulled us further and further apart.

I stopped sharing about my adventures because maybe she thought I was bragging. I stopped sharing photos of my trips because maybe she thought I was bragging. I stopped writing so frequently because maybe she thought I was bragging.

It's the same pattern. Me extending a hand and her spitting on it. Me wanting something more for our relationship and expecting her to oblige. Or at the very least, want the same things.

As much as I hated her at that moment, as much as I wanted to scream at her, I did love her more than anything or anyone else on Earth. At last, Jenna was my sister. I owed it to her to continue trying. It was my duty.

CHAPTER EIGHT

∴

"The worst part about anything that's self-destructive is that it's so intimate. You become so close with your addictions and illnesses that leaving them behind is like killing the part of yourself that taught you how to survive."

Lacy L.

The day Jenna called me was both a surprise and a relief. She said she really needed help and needed to get away from Cain's house.

She asked if she could come stay with me. I was beyond excited, my soul jumping up and down with happiness.

I didn't want to seem overly eager, so I remained neutral and calm on the outside. Eagerness might have scared her off. I agreed, and we discussed how soon she could come, and which airports worked best for her.

Once we got off the phone, I quickly purchased a plane ticket for her to Nashville and emailed the details. Rachel and Delilah seemed fine with my sister visiting. I never disclosed that she was a heroin addict.

I was afraid they would say no if I were completely honest. I couldn't risk that. If Jenna needed to get away from Cain's house, this was my opportunity to reach her. I was going to do whatever I needed to make that happen.

As excited as I was for Jenna to come stay with me, I really had no idea what that meant. I suppose I was living in my own fantasy world about the whole situation.

I figured that Jenna would come, realize Nashville was amazing, and that living together would be fun. This whole drama about addiction and heroin would evaporate somewhere between sightseeing and late-night diner feasts. I was naïve about a lot of things.

I picked Jenna up from the airport with childlike enthusiasm. There were so many things I wanted to show her and share with her. We had so much catching up to do. Now that she was living with me, she couldn't ignore me. She had to be with me.

My mind and expectations got the better of me. The excitement was eradicated just as quickly as it had appeared. I never knew how rapid heroin withdrawals occurred or what that even meant exactly.

Her symptoms started to emerge toward the end of her first day and turned severe by the end of the second day. She was highly restless, shivering with cold, sweating, burning up, angry, irritable, wouldn't eat, wouldn't stop eating, pacing back and forth, sleepless, violent, crying out in pain, aggressive, vomiting, leg cramps, diarrhea, nauseous, and sneezing nonstop.

Most of the time, she would curl up in the fetal position with leg spasms, shivering, sweating, and crying out in pain. It was dizzying and stressful to watch.

I had no idea what to do. I kept asking her if she needed to go to the hospital, but she would refuse. I was powerless, looking over at her in utter pain and misery. Jenna, swaying side-to-side, trying her best to tough it out.

I could almost feel her pain myself. At the very least, my heart ached for her. Watching someone I loved in despair brought me to a dense emotional place.

I wanted to coddle her, like she'd been coddled her entire life. I wanted to soothe her and take away her pain. I felt badly and equally as helpless. There was nothing I could actually do for her. Most of the time, she didn't want to be touched either.

All I could do was watch her and wonder if it was genuine or just a bid for attention. I know withdrawals are intense, but there was no telling just how intense it was with

Jenna and her dramatic demeanor.

I knew I had to be strong for her. Even when she insulted me during her fits of anger, I remained calm and detached. I bought some weed from a coworker to try to relax her nerves. I doubt it even worked for her. Do heroin addicts even feel the effects of weed?

Regardless, she would smoke whatever I got for her. I was afraid to get her anything stronger, assuming it would make matters worse. An old friend told me to get her crack cocaine, but I couldn't bring myself to do that. Helpful or not, weed was where I drew the line.

I was also afraid that Rachel and Delilah would suspect something was going on. Jenna didn't have anything to lose by being at my apartment. I, on the other hand, had everything to lose.

As hard as it was to watch Jenna in such a belittled state, she did put herself there. She had to face the consequences of her actions. This was all her doing.

I know that heroin is bad and highly addictive, but I never knew much more than that. I certainly had no idea about withdrawal symptoms and what that looked like or even how long that process takes.

I guess I was expecting it to be like a cold or bad flu. That once the symptoms were gone, the problem was also gone. It wasn't like that at all though.

I battled with myself over the decision to have her with me. I wasn't even sure I was doing the right thing. She looked like she needed to go to the hospital.

Can you die from heroin withdrawals like alcoholics can? I wasn't even sure when to step in and make the decision to get help for her. Even though she kept refusing professional assistance, I was nervous.

Once, while in Hampi, I got food poisoning. I was sick and in the fetal position for three days. The pain was intense, and I couldn't be more than a few steps from the toilet. I was dehydrated, and my stomach was making gurgling sounds.

Akash forced me to go to the doctor after the third day. He had to pull me from the bed and drag me into his rickshaw. Then he had to force me inside the doctor's house because I didn't want to go. Luckily for me, Akash insisted because I had a parasite and needed medication.

How am I supposed to know when to step in for Jenna? Am I supposed to drag her to the hospital or rehab? Would she ever forgive me if I did? Would I make it worse? There were no answers, only questions and instability.

The withdrawals dragged on much longer than I anticipated. Even though I had no idea what to expect, I assumed it would only take a few days for her to be done with the effects of a detox.

Since it was going on much longer than that, I

wondered if Jenna was, once again, being dramatic. Maybe she was exaggerating for attention or maybe so I would buy her drugs stronger than marijuana.

I was also starting to get annoyed by her and her symptoms. She was restless at night, which meant I wasn't able to get much sleep. Patience has never been one of my characteristics, and neither has weakness.

She was starting to get under my skin. I was exhausted by her and her inability to manage her own life. I was agitated because I now had to step in and suffer because of it.

After a few weeks, the symptoms calmed down, but her urges to get high did not. One day, we were on the bus together, and Jenna saw a woman nodding out from drug use. Jenna nudged me and motioned the woman sitting a few rows in front of us.

"She's high. I wish I felt like that," Jenna confessed.

She paused for a moment allowing herself to savor the yearning as I looked on with utter shock.

"It feels so good," she divulged.

I never even noticed the woman until Jenna pointed her out. She was practically drooling as she continued to shamelessly look on.

I took another peek at this woman. She looked disgusting, dirty and disheveled, her head unsupported and bouncing around. It looked like her head could come loose at any moment as the bus puttered along its route.

The woman's mouth hung open, and her legs were spread apart. Her eyes rolled back into her head. She looked repulsive.

Why on earth would anyone envy that? My sweet, innocent baby Jenna wants to be this dreadful woman? I couldn't even mentally process it. I struggled with that for the rest of the day. Jenna seemed like a stranger to me. A gross, disgusting stranger.

It haunted me as I pretended to be okay. We continued with our day, and I smiled and acted as though I wasn't broken inside. If only Jenna knew, she might be proud.

I'm not Cain, and I would never try heroin to see the allure of it. I couldn't shake how concerned I was for Jenna after that conversation on the bus. I tried my best to empathize, understand, associate, or connect to her desires to be that woman. I kept coming up empty-handed.

The truth was, I was only able to view that woman externally. I was unable to feel the sensation of that experience, the escapism of being high on heroin.

Jenna wanted to escape her body and mind. She was unable to be present or see the value in life. Instead, she preferred to reject life. It broke my heart.

It took effort, but once I overcame my past trauma, I was able to see the beauty of life, the allure and excitement of it. I loved the vastness of life especially once I experienced how good it could be.

I've had the most monumental adventures and wanted to get lost in all the possibilities that life had to offer. Beyond that, I wanted Jenna to feel happy, to live an epic life. I wanted her to finally see the joy in being alive.

I fiercely wished I could get Jenna to that very same place. If only I could bottle up the exhilaration of life and offer her a sip. How do I get her to take a sip of life?

Taking Jenna around town to show her Nashville was really fun for me. It was almost like I finally had the opportunity to travel and explore the world with her. Even though she still wasn't in the best shape with her withdrawals, she went along to all the places I took her.

We visited museums, the main strip at night, cowboy boot and hat shops, restaurants, and local stores. We acted like tourists, taking photos of random things as we carelessly gallivanted around the city.

Happiness and hope radiated through me with each hour that passed. Most of the day, I forgot all about her problems.

She really seemed like she was opening up, too. We would have late-night chats and laugh at almost nothing. We were genuinely reconnecting after all the years of distance. We were both trying our best to have fun and enjoy each moment.

We took many photos together, and she watched on as I playfully posed to entertain her. I felt like a child again. Like we were revisiting our youthful years. I know Jenna wasn't feeling the best, but I was happy.

I figured that all this addiction drama would be over now that Jenna was here with me. We could go on living a normal life together. We could start all over again and we could make up for lost time. This would just be a small blip that we soon forget about.

I had to quit my job at Waffle House. It was exhausting, and the money wasn't worth the struggle. I had to admit to myself that the promise of becoming a manager was nothing more than a weak ploy.

While it did keep me there longer, the outcome was ultimately the same. I found a different waitressing job down the street at LongHorn Steakhouse.

The tips were much better, and the customers were a few steps up. The shifts were longer, sometimes stretching up to twelve hours on a Friday night, but the money was rolling in. It was rare that I walked out with less than $300 on a Friday night.

The other employees had cliques, and it felt a little like high school, but the money was all I cared about. I mostly kept to myself and remained neutral. A few of them were on the meaner side, and I caught them talking about me behind my back.

All that did was solidify the distance I was keeping from them. I still felt disconnected from society in general, and not getting along with my coworkers didn't help. I stayed focused on the purpose of having this job, money.

Eventually, I convinced Jenna to apply for a job at LongHorn Steakhouse. It would be easy and convenient if we worked at the same place.

She agreed, but it didn't seem genuine, almost as if she was just appeasing me. I pushed her a bit on it, though.

She needed a job to stay busy, to have a sense of productivity, connection, and independence. After speaking with my manager, he eagerly agreed to bring her in for an interview.

I told him Jenna was my cousin. I wasn't sure what the policy was on having sisters work together or even on the same shift, and I never took the time to inquire about it.

I had told Jenna about this, and she deflated a bit. I'm not sure why I didn't ask about relatives working together or why I didn't just claim her as my sister. I might have been afraid she wouldn't get the job otherwise. Or that if she got fired it would reflect more poorly on me.

I never meant to hurt her feelings, but I saw that I had. I plowed over her discomfort. I can be too swift sometimes, and Jenna doesn't usually voice her feelings or emotions. It's always been easy for me to overlook her sentiments because of this.

I saw the disappointment on her face about being my cousin, but I figured she'd get over it, that it wasn't a big deal. She might have thought I didn't want to claim her. Perhaps it felt like rejection. But I never took the time to inquire about it.

Once Jenna was done with the interview, she told me she got hired as a hostess. I was beyond elated. It would be incredibly fun to work with her when our shifts collided.

I might even get her to favor my section and send me all the good customers. We immediately ran to the store to buy her a new pair of work pants and shoes.

Even though Jenna never seemed genuinely excited about her new job, I was. I decided to be excited for her. I assumed she was probably just nervous or afraid of being out of New Hampshire.

Jenna had never left the state for longer than a couple weeks, and she had never lived outside Cain's house. So I guess, in that sense, she had never transitioned into adulthood.

Perhaps it was a lot for her to absorb. Perhaps some realities were beginning to sink in, the fact that she was in a new state and about to begin a new chapter, far from the familiarity of Cain.

She was away from all her drug connections and toxic acquaintances. It was time for her to act like an adult and take care of herself. She had never done that before.

Despite seeing her trepidation about starting a new job, I never tried to talk to her about it. I only encouraged her to let go of New Hampshire and try something new.

We all get nervous, and that was normal. Even though Jenna never talked about her feelings, I also never gave her an opportunity to be heard if she wanted to be.

As much as I wanted Jenna to grow up and be an adult, the truth was that she had never done that before. I hated how sheltered she was, and I was sometimes tired and embarrassed by her lack of life accomplishments.

I wanted her to hurry up and get on with life. I never considered how debilitating that can sometimes be for people, especially someone like Jenna. You can't hurry up and be something you've never been before.

The day she was due to start her new job was the same day she left Nashville. Her tax refund check cleared, and she bought the first ticket back to New Hampshire, running straight into Cain's arms. I was devastated.

Jenna never even explained why she was leaving. First, she said she missed Cain. Then she said she was better and no longer needed my help. Then she said she didn't like

Nashville.

What had I missed? Did I push her too hard? Were our disagreements ordinary sibling squabbles, or had I crossed a line that I couldn't see?

What about the progress she had made? She detoxed and was starting to smile again. What about her sobriety? I kept searching my mind for answers to figure it out.

What about the job she was supposed to start? What about us reconnecting? What about all the dreams I had for two sisters traveling and exploring the world together?

I didn't understand how she could just leave. We had just begun a new chapter together and I felt shattered by her decision.

The reality was that my dreams were just mine. She never really wanted any of it. She was pretending for my sake, smiling and pretending it was all okay. I couldn't stop her from leaving, and I wasn't going to try to convince her otherwise either.

I wasn't about to get down on my knees and beg for her to want a better life, or to convince her that my idea of a better life was superior to hers.

Perhaps she got too overwhelmed. Perhaps I glossed over the fact that she was an addict. I tried too hard to force her to be normal. Perhaps that was never a possibility for her.

I failed to give her addiction much attention. In all

honesty, I didn't know I was supposed to. I just assumed it was a minor issue that only needed a quick detox. Since she had done that, we could move on to being normal. Why was she resisting living a regular life?

Jenna left Nashville as swiftly as she had entered it five weeks earlier. Jenna's leaving did offer me some relief. I was anxious about her detoxing around Rachel and Delilah.

I was anxious about leaving her alone in the apartment while I went to work. I was anxious she might steal from me or my roommates.

I was emotionally drained from watching her suffer through detox. I was confused that it didn't fix her problem. I was shattered that she.

I've always had to be the stronger one with Jenna. I always had to take the punches on the chin and keep moving. This time was no different.

She stormed into my Nashville life and rushed right back out of it. I was left disoriented, yet again. I was left feeling defeated and inadequate as a sister, a protector.

I kept replaying those five weeks in my head over and over. What did I miss? What did I fail to say? What did I fail to respond to? What did she try to tell me, but I didn't hear? How could I have been a better sister? How could I have made her stay? The internal torment never wavered.

There was a brief time when Cain separated from his

second family. I was about fifteen years old and Jenna was thirteen. He took us to Las Vegas to blow off some steam. It was our first time, and the city was electric.

Cain often left us to gamble so we had plenty of time to wander around together, marveling at the sites. Both of us awestruck at the lights, buildings, people, and entertainment. Then, an idea came up; let's go bungee jumping.

Jenna and I made a pact to go through with it and Cain offered to pay. We made our way up to the jumping point and Jenna decided to go first. I watched as she walked to the edge of the platform, paused for a moment and leapt.

She hurled herself off with so much confidence you would have assumed she had a pair of wings under her shirt. No fear or retraction, just pure audacity. It was amazing to watch, and I felt proud that she was my sister.

I, on the other hand, almost backed out and could only muster a small bunny hop off the platform. Since Cain paid extra to have it recorded, our differences are immortalized. We gathered many times to rewatch the footage, laughing at how differently we jumped.

Jenna is fearless when it comes to taking dangerous risks. There's no doubt about that. Maybe that's why we are in this position. I wished I was slightly more like her and that she was slightly more like me.

I went to the gym, went to work, went home, and was

in a daze of my own distressed thoughts. I wanted Jenna to be with me. I wanted to give her the opportunity to experience something different, to give her a new perspective on life and its possibilities.

Cain's house was dangerous. It was where souls went to die. I hated that she was back with him. I hated him for allowing it. I hated Jenna for not wanting a better life. I hated Jenna for leaving.

The apartment was getting crowded as Rachel invited her sister to live with us. Rachel and her sister shared one bedroom, me in the other, and Delilah in the living room.

One day, I caught Rachel's sister using the floor cleaner to wash the dishes. That was it. I had spent a lot of time living with other people, and it finally came to a head.

I absolutely needed to be alone. I was drained and on the edge of an intense outburst over those dishes.

I quickly began looking for a new place to stay. I was having a hard time finding something and couldn't wait, so I put my belongings in a storage unit.

I spent a few weeks sleeping in the car that I had recently bought. The apartment had become too intense for me, and I would rather sleep in the car.

Eventually, I found a one-bedroom apartment down the street and moved in. I only had the furniture on loan from Isaac, so the place was bare. That didn't matter because I was alone and very happy to have an entire apartment all to myself.

It's hard to say when the last time I lived alone was. I had always stayed in hostels or with other people while traveling overseas.

There was this one time I stayed in a shed in the backyard of a house while in Australia. It was a metal shed, and it was very hot during the summer, with just a fan to keep me cool.

If you know anything about the summer heat in Australia, you know that a fan is like a drop of water in the ocean, meaningless. I liked staying in the shed because it felt like a private space. I had to go into the main house to use the toilet, shower, and kitchen, which was fine.

The shed came furnished with a bed, nightstand, lamp, desk, and chair. I could only connect to the Wi-Fi when the shed door was open.

It was also the only way to get fresh air, as there were no windows. Most evenings my Australian boyfriend would sneak into the shed after he got off working a late shift.

There was another time when I lived in a crumbling house in Australia with two men from Italy. The men were very intense and would often have screaming matches in the kitchen. I witnessed a few and overheard many.

I started to avoid the kitchen out of fear of getting

caught in the middle of one of their battles. It was always in Italian, so I never knew exactly what they were saying. The rent was cheap at just $300 a month.

The house was infested with mice that would scurry around in the ceiling, especially at night. They had begun to chew holes in the walls to gain access to the house.

One evening, while I was in bed listening to the mice scurry around above me, it sounded like they started to move down the wall. It almost sounded like they were in my room.

Two mice raced across my body as I lay in bed. That was the exact moment I began looking for a new place to live. I've never reached for the light switch or my phone faster in my life.

There was also the time I lived with a guy from the Philippines while in Australia. I lived with him for six months, and we only saw each other three or four times. I loved that I never saw him. He worked during the day, and I worked in the evening.

It was a perfect arrangement, except for the types of food I would find in the fridge, microwave, or oven. He loved everything from chicken feet to fish heads. I never knew what I was about to walk into when entering the kitchen.

Of course, there were the endless hostels I stayed at, some for days, others for months. The rotation of people was always interesting, but the conversations were mundane,

"Where are you from? Where have you visited? How long are you staying in the country?" The typical tourist questions that everyone asks.

The hostel I stayed in the longest, while in Australia, was great because the owner also ran a grocery store. He allowed me to work a few hours a week at his store in exchange for free rent. Usually, I worked the register but sometimes I would stock shelves.

It was a wonderful arrangement until his hostel got shut down by the city. We were all put out within hours of the news, and everyone was upset and anxious about finding new accommodation.

Some kid with rich parents heard about the news and rented an office space. He put a bunch of mattresses on the floor, and about fifteen of us moved in.

It was an odd arrangement living in an office space and sharing such an open area with that many people. It only took a month for the city to catch wind of what was going on before they shut it down, and we were all back to finding new accommodation.

Some of my wildest travel moments were connected to living arrangements. I always tried to find the cheapest places to stay so I could quit meaningless jobs whenever I wanted, leave to travel to other places, or save money.

At last, I was here in Nashville with an apartment of

my own. I signed a one-year lease, which was difficult to do. My hand was shaking while holding the pen to sign.

I wasn't even sure how much longer I wanted to stay in Nashville, but signing a lease made that determination for me.

Traveling is freeing, and signed leases are commitments. I function better with freedom but had to make a temporary sacrifice for the sake of Jenna.

CHAPTER NINE

·∴·

"To love someone in addiction is to love two people in one body: the one that was, and the one that struggles to break free."

Unknown

Mother Mary called me in a panic. Jenna had threatened to kill herself and Mother Mary was certain that she would do it. I tried to brush it off and attribute it to the drama that is Jenna, but Mother Mary wasn't convinced.

I attempted to call Jenna but there was no answer and Mother Mary was frantic. I had no choice but to call into work and explain the situation. I let them know that I needed some time off due to a family emergency.

Well, I actually told them that my aunt had died. I figured that offering such a detail would add to their

sympathy and willingness for me to take a leave of absence. Especially since I couldn't give them an exact return date.

I bought a plane ticket to New Hampshire which was set to leave in only a few hours. I rushed to pack a bag and made my way to the airport. My heart was racing, and I could practically see the excess adrenaline expelling from my mouth.

Mother Mary's voice echoed in my head. Her tone was pure distress. All I could do was hope that nothing happened before I arrived. I rushed through the airport thinking that it would help me get to Jenna sooner.

I wished the plane could time travel and arrive in New Hampshire before the blink of an eye. Sitting in the tiny airplane seat, I could only worry about Jenna and her state of mind.

Worrying that I might not get to her fast enough. Worrying that if she did kill herself, we wouldn't find her right away.

My thoughts went back to Cain and his house. How much of a grasp he had on Jenna. Or was it a spell that he cast upon her? I know Cain's house is bad. Mother Mary knows Cain's house is bad. Why doesn't Jenna know? Maybe she just doesn't want to know.

As soon as I arrived in New Hampshire I picked up a rental car and made my way to Mother Mary's house. We both kept trying to call Jenna to no avail. Mother Mary contacted Cain and he brushed it off as nothing.

He is great at underestimating danger. He'll minimize the collapse of the world and gaslight you into believing that you are the crazy one as humanity topples before your very eyes. It's equally fascinating as it is terrifying.

Jenna was nowhere to be found. She might have been hiding at Cain's house, and he was covering for her. Who knows. We sure as hell didn't.

Mother Mary and I regrouped and decided to wait until the following morning to investigate things further. I fell asleep on the sofa while watching TV. I needed sound to distract from my racing thoughts.

The next day, Mother Mary got in contact with Jenna. It was the usual conversation with Jenna going back on her own words and taking a page out of Cain's playbook. She tried to manipulate the situation and make Mother Mary feel as though she were exaggerating.

"Stop making it a thing. Why is everything a huge deal with you?" Jenna questioned in an attempt to deflect from the situation.

The way that she tried to downplay her previous threats was infuriating. I'm sorry but threatening to kill yourself to your own mother and then acting as though she's making it a big deal is genuinely insane. Yet, Mother Mary and I didn't buy it for a second. We weren't going away that easily.

We hatched a plan to lore Jenna to us. We tricked Jenna into agreeing to have dinner under the guise that I was in town visiting. Jenna took the bait.

She agreed to meet us later that evening for dinner and she even chose the restaurant. We thought that having Jenna pick the location was a nice touch to the plan.

It was after 7 o'clock and Mother Mary and I picked Jenna up. The restaurant she chose was on the way to our real destination, so Jenna wasn't suspicious at first. We acted normal as we drove past the restaurant without slowing down. Jenna chimed in,

"Weren't we supposed to go to that restaurant you just passed?"

"Oh, gosh. Did I pass it? My bad," Mother Mary said nonchalantly.

"Yeah, just turn around up there," Jenna requested, gesturing ahead.

Mother Mary kept driving without slowing down. Jenna, sitting in the front seat, perked up as she realized that we were not going out to dinner.

"What's going on? What are we doing? Answer me!" Jenna yelped.

Mother Mary and I both remained quiet. We never

actually thought about this part. At least we never discussed it with each other during the planning stage.

Jenna was starting to panic and by panic I actually mean, freak out. She was thrashing in her seat and slamming her feet on the dashboard.

Terror washed over me as her aggression turned into violence. As she was thrashing, she was also screaming. At times she was saying things and other times she was just screaming.

It was bloodcurdling. It reminded me of Jenna when she was little. Her temper tantrums were of epic proportion.

I had never seen anyone in my life act like this let alone my sweet, innocent baby Jenna. She was cursing and threatening to kill herself along with us. She was crying and punching the dashboard, pulling at her own hair and punching herself in the head.

My nerves were through the roof. What if she grabs the steering wheel? I'll be forced to take her out in some way. At least I'll have the advantage of being behind her. She can't see me too well and I could easily choke her out if she puts us in danger.

I felt like I was witnessing a body become possessed by a demon. Or a demon showing its well-established possession of a body.

Either way, it was not of this world. Jenna persisted to

thrash around, scream, cry, beg, plead, threaten and stomp as we continued to drive north.

I watched on in horror. It was the ugliest and scariest thing I have ever witnessed. Beads of sweat were falling down my face as I prepared for whatever was about to come.

I might have to choke my baby sister. I might have to hurt her in order to save Mother Mary and me. These brand-new thoughts pulsated through my brain.

Our car came up to a traffic light that turned yellow. Fear flashed through me and raised the hair on my body. Mother Mary drives like a grandma. Yellow lights only mean one thing.

"Keep going. Don't you dare stop at that light," I ordered, frantic and fearful of Jenna's current state.

There was silence as Mother Mary thought about what she was going to do. I could see her contemplating the options and what the results of her options would be. The roads were empty, there were no traffic cameras, and we were in a small town.

She needed to run the light. She's the type that drives under the speed limit. The ones that drive you crazy as you eventually pass them on a double yellow line and curse.

As I felt the car slow, I insisted with urgency, *"Don't do it. Don't you dare stop at that light."*

Mother Mary didn't listen and stopped at the now

red light. It wasn't surprising what happened next. Jenna opened the car door, jumped out, and began running down the middle of the street.

She was running toward Cain's house, crying and flailing her arms in a state of weakened distress. She used up all her energy thrashing and screaming in the car, and now she was attempting to flee without any endurance.

"What did I fucking say?!" I hissed.

I jumped out of the car and quickly chased after her. I felt like I was in a dream, a nightmare. My body felt odd from the adrenaline and tension. I caught up to her, grabbed the hood of her sweatshirt, and jerked, bringing her down to the ground.

A struggle ensued as my body went numb. Jenna and I had never gotten into a physical fight before, at least not one that was anything more than a push. It felt like an out-of-body experience.

One time, when we were younger, we got into an argument. Jenna came at me with a pair of scissors. I dodged out of the way and then shoved her as hard as I could.

She fell backward onto some shelving and bruised her back. Jenna went and spun some fairytale story to Mother Mary, making me the attacker.

Mother Mary forced me into therapy after that. She said I was violent and dangerous, that I needed psychological help. I went to therapy once a week for six months for that. Imagine nearly being attacked and then being made the perpetrator.

I never said a word to the therapist. We would sit there in absolute silence for the entire hour. I was angry that I was the scapegoat.

I was also afraid. I knew I couldn't tell the truth about the abuse. Unless Jenna and I were taken away immediately, it would have to remain a secret.

The therapist would try to manipulate me into talking. Little did she know, she was actually an amateur at manipulation. All her tactics were child's play.

I had been manipulated my entire life by a beast of a human. I was always the bad one. I was always to blame for everything. Sweet, innocent Jenna could never do wrong.

Jenna and I rumbled in the middle of the street as I got on top of her, punched her, and forced her into submission. The animal part of me wanted to draw blood. The sister in me just wanted her to stop torturing herself and us along with her.

Mother Mary came running up to us and screamed for us to stop. I still have an automatic fear response to Mother Mary, especially when she gets aggressive.

I jumped back and threw my hands up as if she were armed with a gun. She and I quickly gathered Jenna, who burst into tears, as we placed her back into the car.

Mother Mary listened to me as she drew closer to the next traffic light, which was yellow and about to turn red. Thank God. I really don't think I could have been as nice about it if I had to wrestle her again.

Jenna was half in a rage and half in a nervous breakdown. Tossing and turning in the front seat, yelling, cursing, and banging her feet against the floorboards.

Mother Mary and I thought she was being hyper-dramatic and acting like a baby. Who thrashing in a car as they are being driven to their mother's house? I couldn't help but wonder if Jenna was mentally deranged.

It was in this car ride that I realized something. Whatever was happening with Jenna, was beyond me, Mother Mary, or Cain. This wasn't something that was going to go away after a few weeks in Nashville. Fear swept over my body and my stomach dropped with this realization.

The reality was that we were taking Jenna away from her heroin supply, which meant she would soon start experiencing withdrawal symptoms. She panicked and reacted violently at the imminent fear of the pain that came alongside that. A reaction that didn't seem proportionate to her behavior.

We were all still reeling from the events that had just transpired as the car pulled into Mother Mary's driveway.

Jenna needed to be escorted, so Mother Mary took her arm and guided her inside. The plan was to get Jenna to Mother Mary's house.

We just needed to get her away from Cain. We needed to know why she threatened to commit suicide. One thing was very clear: Mother Mary and I would never be successful burglars or kidnappers.

I may sometimes fantasize about robbing a bank vault in the middle of the night, but my planning skills are less than mediocre. I could figure out the beginning, but after that, I forget to consider the various outcome possibilities.

I like to imagine that I was a professional heist person in a previous life; however, if I were, none of those skills had transferred to this current life. It was my best effort, considering that this was my very first kidnapping. If you want to call it that.

All three of us gathered at the interrogation table once again. Jenna downplayed the situation and was aggressive in her disdain for our kidnapping plan. On one hand, we did force her to come here, but on the other hand, she did threaten to kill herself.

What exactly were we supposed to do? Ignore it? Chalk it up to her being dramatic? Wait to be contacted once she went through with it and killed herself?

We really weren't left with many options. We were

fighting for Jenna's life. Whether she liked it or not. Whether she was with us or not.

Jenna couldn't sit at the table for very long. She was highly irritated and aggressive. She reached for her phone and dialed Cain. Jenna really did miss her calling as an actress.

If life had been different, she would have easily been a highly acclaimed actress. The moment Cain picked up the phone, she switched into her Oscar-worthy performance.

"Please come get me Daddy," she urged as if no one else could hear the conversation.

"I just want to go home," Jenna continued as she avoided making eye contact with me.

I watched as she forced herself to cry and play the role as an innocent victim. She went on to tell Cain that we had kidnapped her and that she wanted to call the police.

She begged him to come get her. Jenna claimed that she was afraid for her life. She must have used the word *"daddy"* three dozen times.

I sat in disgust as I listened. It's an odd place to be internally, to love and hate someone at the same time. I often couldn't differentiate which side was more dominant.

At that moment, I hated her. I hated everything about her. More than that, I hated how she tormented Mother Mary and me. So callous and recklessly breaking our hearts without a second thought.

Jenna passed the phone to Mother Mary, who walked into the other room, out of earshot. I was staring at Jenna, wondering how she was able to switch like that, how she could play the innocent victim while she uprooted everyone's life around her. Right now, my hatred was clearly winning. It was winning by a lot.

I almost wished I had the opportunity to choke her on the car ride over. What a selfish bitch to tell Mother Mary that she wanted to kill herself and then cry when we responded.

What a selfish bitch to drown us all in her misery. What a selfish bitch to cry on demand and manipulate family.

I wanted to shake her. To grab her shoulders and shake them. Maybe we would both wake up and realize this was all a dream.

Maybe we would both wake up in India and go down by the river to watch the elephant get bathed. I desperately wished that was the case. However, this is not a dream. This nightmare is my reality.

Mother Mary re-entered the main area and explained to Jenna that Cain would pick her up in the morning, that she would be staying the night. Jenna threw an absolute temper tantrum. She screamed in rage, punched a hole in the living room wall, then wailed out in pain and ran off to the spare bedroom, slamming the door.

Jenna is no stranger to temper tantrums. When we

were children, she used to do it regularly. She would hold her breath and turn blue if she didn't get her way.

These were some of my earliest memories. Jenna throwing a fit, holding her breath, and turning blue. We used to scream at her,

"Breathe!"

"Breathe, Jenna!"

Sometimes she would pass out, and sometimes she would get hit in an attempt to make her cry. She was even taken to the doctor for her tantrums.

The doctor said it was fine and to smack her or lightly bite her so that she would cry and start breathing again. A born drama queen, and never anything else.

Mother Mary and I both sat on the couch in silence. We were stunned, confused, and distressed. What were we supposed to do? How do you help someone who doesn't want help? How do you save someone who doesn't want to be saved? Mother Mary got up and went to bed.

I was left on the couch with the TV on but no processing capabilities to hear the sounds it was making. I was left deaf with despair.

If nothing was working, then how do I know when it's time to surrender? Maybe now was the time. She wanted to die but still doesn't want help.

Perhaps the demon that had her was preventing her

from accepting help. Perhaps we are up against a demon. How do you battle one of those?

I left New Hampshire after several days and many attempts to get Jenna into some kind of help. We were never able to get through to her, and leaving felt like a failure once again. I was belittled and felt like the worst sister alive. I failed her again, and I was leaving her again.

I was embarrassed to call myself a sister, and even worse, an older sister. Someone who was supposed to be a support. A guiding light.

I desperately wanted to leave the US. I wanted to run away from all of it. The confusion, the exhaustion, the instability.

Yet, my guilty conscience wouldn't allow me to further abandon Jenna. I had to remain strong and stay within the country. If anything were to happen to her, I would never be able to forgive myself.

CHAPTER TEN

∴

"Intentional or not, I was being taught that my discomfort was unimportant and that the potential of upsetting another outweighed my own feelings."
Michelle Elman

I jumped up from bed, covered in sweat, my heart racing. Another nightmare. It was the same one that had been occurring two or three times a week.

In the nightmare, I'm entering what looks like a McDonald's restaurant. I walk through the side door and go directly into the ladies' bathroom. Once I open the restroom door, I see Jenna sitting on the floor with her back against the wall.

Her head is dropped to the side, and her skin is discolored. A piece of blue rubber is wrapped around her bicep, and a needle hangs from her arm. I grab her shoulders and shake her.

I scream her name and shake her again. Nothing happens, and I begin to panic, screaming louder and shaking harder.

This was always the point when I would jump up from bed, drenched in sweat. My pillow and sheets were also soaked. My heart raced as I burst into tears. Out of pure fear, I usually grabbed my phone to check if I had missed any calls or texts from Jenna.

It was tormenting me to the point where I didn't even want to sleep. I was deathly afraid of sleep since this nightmare had been haunting me regularly. Sometimes, I went to the gym at the apartment complex and walked on the treadmill or lifted weights instead.

When I did manage to sleep, it was from sheer exhaustion. The days felt endless, and the nights were pure hell. I never knew if it was day or night or what I was supposed to be doing.

I was a zombie at work, forgetting orders, drinks, and tabs. Whenever I forgot an order, I blamed it on the kitchen staff, and the customers seemed to believe it. I was nothing but an empty shell, a soulless entity that existed for no reason.

I felt as though I wasn't even in my body most of the time. It felt like I was watching a movie rather than living a life. Has time frozen? Could anyone see me?

My thoughts were consumed by Jenna, the agony I felt, and the doom of my recurring nightmare. The dread of what was to come enveloped me at all hours of the day and night. Sometimes, I thought I caught a glimpse of the Grim Reaper out of the corner of my eye.

I could swear it was him, lurking and stalking me. He wasn't after me, though. I knew that. His eyes were fixated on Jenna, the only person in the world that I loved. The only person I would die for.

Despite that fact that his image and reputation were beastly, I wasn't afraid. I would fight him if need be. I would challenge and thwart his mission, if necessary. He could follow me around all day and night if he wanted. He could observe me suffering, but that suffering wouldn't weaken my determination.

Isaac started coming to the LongHorn restaurant more regularly. He would sit in my section with the hope and assumption that we would catch up. This job was different from the Waffle House, as my section was larger, and I had more tables to tend to.

There was much less time to talk with him, but he would still show his support. I always gave him an employee discount, too. I think that's part of the reason why he would visit.

The prices were much higher at LongHorn so the

discount helped. Isaac had always supported me since my very first night in Nashville. It was the least I could do.

More often, we would meet at Waffle House or Cracker Barrel with a few of the other gentlemen from their friend group. It was quite fun to hang out with southern men in their seventies and eighties.

They were polite, friendly, and their accents always made me chuckle to myself. They would perpetually pay for my food and get mad if I ever tried to offer to pay. It was really nice and comforting to have these gentlemen in my life.

Being around them was one of the only times I felt normal. I felt like I could relax, converse, laugh, and enjoy the company of others. Jenna was never on my mind when I was with the southern gentlemen.

I was always present and felt loved. It was a wonderful opportunity for me to escape my thoughts. I always savored our outings.

Once they found out about the new apartment I had moved into, they all gathered more furniture for me to borrow. I was given a kitchen table with chairs, dishes, a convection oven, pots and pans, glassware, cutlery, blankets, and a shelf for the bathroom.

Their generosity left me speechless each time. I almost felt as though I wasn't worthy of it, like I wasn't deserving of good fortune. Receiving has never been my strong suit. A lady should be accustomed to receiving gracefully, so perhaps this was my opportunity to process and work through that.

On an ordinary and unsuspecting day, Jenna called me in a panic. Whenever she called, I would pick up the phone before it even completed the first ring. I was on edge from my nightmare and non-stop obsessive thoughts of her. I assumed every call from her was a last goodbye.

When I answered the phone, she was frantic, rushed, and demanding. She hastily explained that she wanted to get clean. She was done with heroin, and she meant it this time.

She promised things would be different if I allowed her to come detox in Nashville again. Jenna promised she would do better.

Granted, these words were the sweetest thing you could possibly hear from an addict, I had heard them before. Many times. My spirits no longer lifted from receiving them. It was true that my optimism had been depleted, yet I wondered if this could be the moment.

This could be the moment that Jenna's addiction gets resolved. It could be the last time I had to hear her cries for help. I couldn't say no to her. I could never say no to Jenna when she asked for help.

This time, I offered a bus ticket rather than a flight. She wanted to immediately come to Nashville that night, but the cost of the flight was too much, especially considering last time.

She fought with me over the bus ticket. It would take days to get to Nashville by bus, and she would already be detoxing from heroin by then.

I stayed strong with my offer, and she angrily hung up. I didn't understand her. I had been trying to help her for months. I had extended many offers to her. I had hosted her in Nashville before. Here she was, demanding that I buy her a plane ticket to leave that night.

It was close to $1,000, but what did she care? It wasn't her money. Everyone had always picked up her messes and bowed to her demands. Her lack of gratitude and respect pissed me off. That's what happens when you spoil children. They become spoiled adults.

Jenna called me back a few hours later. Cain had offered to buy her a plane ticket, and she would leave the following morning. Jenna was resourceful, to say the least.

Or maybe she just had a few people under her spell. You really only needed a few people to go along with your every demand.

She always seemed to get whatever she wanted, no matter the circumstances or consequences. Since I didn't have the same experience, it was sometimes difficult to be happy for her.

There was virtue in self-reliance, not in manipulation. Nonetheless, I was happy she wanted to come stay with me. I was happy she wanted help. I was happy for this whole thing to end.

Yet, there was something that bothered me. Her extreme urgency to come to Nashville. She insisted on coming immediately. Why did it have to be so quickly?

She tried to get me to buy her a plane ticket for that very same day. Rudeness aside, why was it so urgent? It was odd.

Something definitely seemed off. I also don't have much patience, but demanding that people help you, dictating how they help and in what timeframe, is rather extravagant. Either way, I had an opportunity to get through to her. The more space between her and Cain, the better.

I picked Jenna up from the airport, and we went straight to the grocery store. I wanted her to pick out whatever food she desired. Especially now that I had my own place, we could get anything and not worry about shared spaces.

I wanted her detox to be as comfortable as possible, and having the foods and drinks that she wanted seemed like a good thing to do.

The car I had purchased was an old 2005 Honda Civic. It was cute, and I loved Hondas. They were such reliable cars and easy to fix too. Any backyard mechanic could fix a Honda

Civic.

Since my credit score was still low, I had to buy it from one of those car dealers that offer financing with weekly payments.

I didn't get the best deal on the car, but it was mine. I had the freedom to come and go as I pleased. I would even sometimes drive around late at night when I was afraid to go to sleep, just because I could.

Having my own car also helped with Jenna being here. We had more freedom and didn't need to rely on public transportation. We could explore a wider radius of the city and its surrounding suburbs, too.

Having a job with more tips meant that I had more money around the house. I made sure to hide some of it and put the majority in the bank. Not only did I not trust Jenna very much, but I also didn't want to tempt her.

Nashville had a lot of bad areas, and there was drug usage around the city. Out of sight was out of mind. At least, I hoped so this time around.

Jenna was in good spirits the first day. She seemed excited and happy to be with me and more comfortable now that I had my own apartment. I bought an air mattress before she arrived and put it on the floor in the bedroom.

She and I took turns sleeping on it. It was hard to sleep next to someone who was detoxing. She was absolutely restless and sweat a ton.

To make it fair, some days I would take the air mattress, and she would take the bed. Just so it was even, and we were both comfortable.

The first week was hard to manage. It felt worse than the last time she detoxed at my house. Maybe because we had the apartment to ourselves, she felt more comfortable being vocal or aggressive. Sometimes her moods were unbearable. She seemed more restless this time around too. Her legs were moving non-stop, and she was sneezing a lot more.

She often complained about having cramps in her legs, and she couldn't stop moving them. It's called restless leg syndrome, and it's common with opioid withdrawals.

I have never experienced this myself, but Jenna made it look intense. It gets worse at night and when lying down or sitting. It causes sleep deprivation and general distress.

The higher the dose of heroin a person uses, the more common and intense restless leg syndrome becomes during withdrawals. As much as I wanted to take away her pain, there was nothing I could do for her. I could only stay close and witness her journey.

It was often difficult for me to sleep with the movements and sounds coming from Jenna. All I could do was listen to her anguish. I couldn't reduce the sensation. I couldn't eliminate the symptoms.

I felt like a villain just being there and not making her any better. She used to comfort me when we were children. How do I comfort her now?

I was trying to remain strong for her, but there's only so much a person can take. Her aggressive outbursts were becoming insulting and hurtful. They would come out of nowhere, and she would often snap at me for nothing.

I tried my best to balance being compassionate with enforcing boundaries. It was challenging. I also felt bound to be more obliging because I didn't want her to leave.

I know she was in a lot of pain. A pain I will never understand, but it is a pain she deserved. A pain she bestowed upon herself. A pain that was all her fault.

How much compassion could I really have for her? This was all her own doing. She didn't want to go to rehab where they would offer her medication to ease the symptoms. They could also support her and understand what she was going through.

I felt extremely inadequate. She insisted on coming here. She knew what she was getting herself into. It was a double-edged sword for me.

I loved her, and yet, that familiar hatred was beginning to surface again. Jenna's suffering was now my suffering.

Jenna's angst was now my angst. Jenna's drug problem was now my drug problem. All I wanted was for her to get professional help and for her addiction to go away.

She controlled it. She was the one who could make it stop. She could stop all of our suffering. Yet, she was refusing and I now had to suffer even more.

I had to witness her detox again and bear the brunt of her emotional dysregulation. I could hardly handle my own emotions, let alone those of others.

There were several nights that things seemed to spiral or get too intense. She either appeared to be in too much pain or was getting too aggressive. I couldn't help but remember her coming at me with that pair of scissors when we were growing up.

I became afraid of her on several occasions, so I suggested taking her to the hospital. She scoffed at the recommendation. I wasn't about to bring up going to a rehab again either, so I left it alone. I knew I was out of my league, and I began to feel hopeless. Perhaps I was even more lost than Jenna.

"I've already been to rehab. I know everything they are going to say. I don't need to go there again," she would insist.

I couldn't complain much because at least she was with me. Away from Cain and his house. Away from heroin and her drug contacts. It was small but it was something.

I continued to purchase marijuana for her to ease the symptoms. I thought about buying something stronger, but again, I decided not to.

I had a small balcony off the living room in the apartment. She would smoke weed and cigarettes there, making it easier for her when she had late-night urges.

I tried to keep the kitchen stocked with any snacks or drinks she liked. Her eating was sporadic, and I wanted to make her as comfortable as possible. It felt like it was all I could do.

Jenna and I had better days after that first week, it was far less intense. After two weeks, we started to have fun together.

We would explore the city, eat at restaurants, cruise the streets in the evening, go thrift shopping in the rich suburbs, and share sisterly laughs in the dead of night.

I was really happy to have her next to me. I loved her so much and only wanted her to flourish. I wanted to be done with this addiction. I wanted to start living with her in health and happiness.

Jenna also started to open up to me more this time around. She shared some darker details about her addiction, details that weren't easy to hear. She shared that she had overdosed several times and was actually shocked that she hadn't already died.

I was in disbelief when I heard that and felt an emptiness in the pit of my stomach. I kept thinking about my recurring nightmare and the intensity of it. My ultimate fear of losing Jenna. It was closer to reality than I wanted to admit.

I never wanted to force her to share any details, but I also wanted her to feel safe to open up to me. For that reason, I had to stay as neutral as possible and keep my emotions to myself. It was hard to hide my anxiety and distress, but I forced myself to anyway.

The fact that Jenna was shocked she was still alive spoke volumes about how little I really knew about her addiction, and how far she had gone into it.

I wondered if Cain knew. I wondered if he was one of the people who had brought her back to life without ever speaking a word of it.

Jenna confessed that she had prostituted herself many times for heroin. I wasn't sure which one of those details was harder to absorb: not only was she a junkie, but she was a hooker, too.

Her admissions were overwhelming and tested my sense of reality. My mind desperately wanted to reject what she was saying because it was impossible.

My sweet, innocent baby Jenna was no longer sweet or innocent in the eyes of the world or God, if there was one.

She also revealed that she had contracted hepatitis C from sharing needles. A junkie, a hooker, and an idiot. I felt sick to my stomach.

I couldn't help but think that she should have been placed into quarantine. I wanted to hug her, but my body recoiled. She was a dirty stranger.

There was a treatment for hepatitis C, but when Jenna inquired about it, she was told that she needed to be clean for a minimum of six months before being considered for it. Jenna had never been eligible because she had never been clean for that long in close to a decade.

Hepatitis C was fatal, but I never got the feeling that she was too worried about it. She assumed heroin would kill her long before hepatitis C had a chance. I'm sure it was low on the ranking score of priorities for her.

Growing up, Mother Mary always worked several jobs which meant that she wasn't around too much.

One morning before school, Jenna cut her finger. She ran over to me with blood dripping down her arm. I took her to the bathroom, washed the cut and placed a band-aid over it.

I told her to have it looked at by the nurse once we got to school. I wish life was still that simple. I wish I could patch Jenna up and send her on her way.

During her confession, she continued to share that she

had taken over the drug route of her main supplier. He had been arrested for dealing and was in jail, awaiting sentencing.

Jenna visited him and got his blessing to take over the route. She informed me that she had done pick-ups for him in the past and already knew most of his connections and suppliers.

The more she spoke, the more I felt like it wasn't real. It had to be a nightmare. There was no way Jenna was capable of this. I rubbed my eyes and shook my shoulders to check. Nope, it was not a nightmare. This was real.

With each new piece of information, more aspects of my reality broke away. The person that I knew was not there anymore.

The curly haired little girl that I played with and told all my secrets too was no longer alive. Worst yet, I had no idea when she died. The shift forced me to disassociate from myself. These stories were the true depths of Jenna, and it was heart-wrenching.

My mind wandered as I recalled all the movies, TV series, and documentaries I'd seen about drug lords, the cartel, small-time dealers, drug wars, trap houses, and everything else that went along with that underbelly world.

I imagined Jenna in a dirty stash house surrounded by guns, doped-out baggers, and guards at the front door. It was too impossible for my mind to believe. I refused to believe that

Jenna was doing any of it. She had to be lying. I desperately wanted her to be lying.

As her older sister, I remained neutral yet inquisitive. Though, my heart sank to the floor, and I felt different about her. I felt severed. She was not who I thought I knew. This person in my house was not my baby Jenna but rather an unknown and nameless drifter

How did life get so far off course? How did she become so lost? How did I not know the extent of her journey into darkness? At what point do you accept people for who they are today rather than who they were yesterday?

I wondered if I was living in a fantasy, if by hoping and pressuring her to get sober, I wasn't doing it for her at all. I wondered if it was only me attempting to recreate the old Jenna that I used to know. Was I just unwilling to accept her for who she had chosen to become?

I should have checked in with her more. I should have forced her to be around me. What a crazy thought, forcing someone to be with you or to open up to you. I was convinced I could have done it. That a good older sister would have found a way.

After that conversation, I tried my best to put aside the details of Jenna's addiction. I tried to pretend that it was either fake or a part of her that no longer existed, a small, dark patch that she could instantly detach from.

In actuality, all I was doing was glazing over reality in a vain attempt to make myself feel better, to offer myself some sort of hope for the future.

To pretend that there was still my sweet, innocent baby Jenna inside the body that stood before me. I tried to do what Jenna would have wanted and smiled while pretending that everything was okay.

As the days and weeks progressed, we continued to spend time together. I took Jenna to see the Gaylord Opry House. It's a fantastic place that feels like a dream. Technically, it's a resort and convention center, but really, it's so much more than that.

They have an outdoor waterpark, an indoor waterpark, a hotel, twelve restaurants, over four acres of indoor gardens, an indoor river you can ride along in a boat, spas, a golf course, pool parties, shopping, and much more. It's probably my favorite place in the city to wander around.

Jenna had always loved plants and gardening. She even worked at a garden nursery for several years. I took her to the Gaylord Opry House to wander around the majestic indoor atrium.

I suggested that she get a job there. It would be an amazing place to work, and she could be indoors while still working with plants.

After a little convincing, she agreed to it. One of the

biggest things I disliked about Jenna was her nonexistent self-worth. She didn't value herself at all, and she didn't believe she was capable of new or great things. It showed the most when she was faced with anything unfamiliar.

If I could change one thing about her, it would be that. I would remove it and absorb it myself if that were possible. Just the thought of her living in a new place and getting a job in such a huge facility had her melting with anxiety and doubt.

I was there to support her, though, and part of support involves being present while they explore unfamiliar territory.

That evening, we jumped online and filled out an application. I was excited. This was really happening. Things were different this time around.

At least that's what I thought at that moment. It wasn't long before things drastically changed. It wasn't long before my foolish optimism imploded in my face.

Jenna and I were in the bedroom. She was frantic, practically flailing around like a fish out of water. I watched her squirm with disdain. I hated her. She had decided that she no longer wanted to be in Nashville.

For the past two days, she had attempted to beg, bully, and victimize her way into a plane ticket back to New Hampshire. I wouldn't budge. I told her that if she wanted to go back, she would need to find her own way. I wasn't going to support it.

The day before, I called Cain while I was alone and, on my way, to work. I explained that Jenna was begging to go back and that I needed him to align with me. I needed him to refuse to help her.

Surprisingly, he agreed. He shared how much worse Jenna had gotten and that he was frustrated with her and her behavior.

This might be the break that Mother Mary and I needed: Cain being frustrated and no longer desiring Jenna in his house. This would work to our advantage for sure. After Cain agreed, we ended the call.

When Jenna called Cain in utter distress, begging to go home, I smiled to myself. I had already spoken with him, and I beat her to it. Cain stayed true to his word and refused to help Jenna find a way back to New Hampshire.

It was equally disgusting and impressive to watch Jenna switch her manipulation tactics in the blink of an eye. Her acting skills making another appearance. She would start off as a victim in distress, then move on to crying.

Next, she would try aggression. Finally, she would switch into a child and call Cain, *"Daddy."* It was a rollercoaster to witness.

"Please, can I come home? I really need to come home now. I'm clean. I haven't had any drugs. I swear, things are

different now," Jenna pleaded as she paced around my bedroom.

"But you don't understand, I don't have any money. Please, I just need a plane ticket to go home tonight. I miss you," she begged with exhaust and surrender.

"Why are you doing this to me? You hate me! You have to buy the ticket NOW!!" she demanded as her arms swung in frustration.

"Please, Daddy. Please. I love you, Daddy. I just want to be with you. I just want to come home," she cried, plopping down on my bed in resolve. The tone of her voice softened as she switched to being more childlike.

I practically threw up in my mouth, watching the unraveling of a codependent latch. Did she even realize how disgusting she looked? Being an addict, I'm sure this was on the lesser end of the disgusting meter for her. Who was this person in my house?

This devil-monster that rips through your life, destroys everything in sight, and then screams as it exits. This monster cares nothing about your heart and is happy to rip it out of your chest, throw it on the floor, stomp on it, stab it a few times with a knife, then look you in the eyes and cry victim.

I wished she had never tried drugs. I sometimes wished she had never existed at all. All she does is cause pain and turmoil.

I could deal with having less of that. After no success with Cain, Jenna quickly moved on to other contacts in her phone.

She called person after person until she finally got a bite. One of her drug connections seemed to go along with her pleas for help. She was very determined to get exactly what she desired. The cost of covering these desires was not her concern.

"*I really need your help,*" Jenna requested as she sat at the edge of my bed, feet perched on the side of the bed frame. Her hair was in a messy bun and the bottom of her loose sweatpants draped over her feet.

"*I need you to buy me a plane ticket from Nashville to New Hampshire,*" she informed the person on the other end of the call.

"*No, it needs to be tonight,*" she insisted.

"*You have no idea. It's horrible here. Please, help me,*" she begged as her voice switched to a tone of urgency and distress. Her face tightened and her forehead wrinkled as she prepared to release a few tears.

"*Okay, I'll do it. Whatever. I just need to get out of here right now,*" she agreed. "*It's torture being here,*" she added.

"*Thank you. Thank you. You have no idea how much*

you saved me," she affirmed. Her body softened with relief as her shoulders relaxed away from her ears.

She hung up the phone and texted him the details for the ticket. Her fake tears seemed to have evaporated right before my very eyes. What a bitch. Did she really just say all of those things right in front of me?

Absolutely no regard for my feelings. She didn't even have the decency to take the call outside. I hated her. What an absolute bitch.

I was tired of her shit. All she did was stomp on me, then smile as she walked away, leaving me to pick up the pieces. I watched her detox in my apartment, ate all the food and drinks I had purchased for her, and smoked all the weed I had supplied.

She ate at all the restaurants I had taken her to, drank all the coffee I bought her, borrowed clothing from my closet, ran up my electric and water bills, and happily burned the gas in my car as we went sightseeing.

And she had the gall to insult me. She had the gall to make me feel like a loser for sheltering her. She could figure out her own way to the airport, as far as I was concerned.

I am a strong person. I am capable of withstanding many things. Disrespect in my own house, however, was not one of them. I sat in utter silence and watched this monster in my house.

Sleeping in my bed, using my towels, cooking on my pans. This monster, once someone I loved deeply, but no longer recognized. At what point are you considered an only child? Does their soul have to leave Earth, or does their body also need to leave?

Jenna left just as quickly as she entered my Nashville life. My recurring nightmare of finding Jenna in the McDonald's bathroom continued, and so did my torment. I avoided Mother Mary's calls.

I no longer wanted to be Jenna's keeper, the in-between person who had to experience pain from both sides. I no longer wanted to come running when Jenna cried. I no longer wanted her to come stay with me. I no longer wanted to participate in the insanity.

I regretted leaving India. I regretted upending my life for someone who didn't care about me in return. Fuck her and her addiction. Whatever happened to her was her own doing.

Whatever her fate was, that was between her and God or the Universe. Not me. Even though hate ran through my veins, the inner torment continued. The guilt remained. I ruminated on the past.

At some point, Jenna's despair became my own. I was the one drowning now. The only difference was that there was no one who would save me.

No calls for help to be made. Jenna was the spotlight.

I was in darkness. No one focuses on the darkness when there's a spotlight to witness.

I felt alone and isolated. I felt abandoned and rejected all over again. I felt that I wasn't good enough or worthy enough of interest or compassion. I was tossed to the side and never given a second glance.

When I was in elementary school, my guidance counselor suggested that I write a letter to Mother Mary to express my feelings. She thought it was a good alternative to talking with her since you can't really say much to Mother Mary without her flying into a rage.

I was petrified but I trusted my guidance counselor and wrote it with a trembling hand. I wrote how I felt left out, neglected and unloved. I poured my little heart out as it raced in my chest. I then placed the letter on Mother Mary's pillow and waited.

Several days passed without a single word. Being the naïve child that I was, I wrote a second letter. The first letter must have gotten lost or blown away in the wind, I thought.

I did my best to rewrite the letter and placed it on her pillow, again. Later that day Mother Mary, with letter in hand, came rushing towards me and proclaimed, *"Another one of your stupid notes?"*

My heart raced but I tried my best to be brave. I just wanted her to know that I felt unloved. That I felt insignificant. That I needed her. The way she scoffed at me with all my emotions written on the paper that she clinched in her fist, broke my heart. This moment was a turning point for me.

I realized that I was never going to matter because she didn't care. I needed to harden my heart to preserve it. I had to keep people out so that they wouldn't reject me.

I also stopped trusting my guidance counselor because she put me in danger and the outcome of her suggestion left me more hurt than before.

Here I was, all these years later feeling the exact same way, rejected by Mother Mary. Left to be outcast and ignored.

The truth was that she had never cared much for me. Jenna had always been her favorite. Her prized possession.

Jenna had always been everyone's main concern. Jenna and her victimized state. It sure was a tactic that worked.

No one was interested in me, my pain, or my glory. Why would they, when Jenna was holding her breath and turning blue.

CHAPTER ELEVEN

.·.

"You may not control all the events that happen to you, but you can decide not to be reduced by them."

Maya Angelou

The days muddled into weeks, and then months. It all just felt like a rerun: wake up, go to the gym, shower, change, go to work, go home, sleep, repeat. My body was numb, and I felt empty, depleted. I walked around in a detached state of mind.

My body was at work, but my mind was not. I was nothing more than a robot performing pre-programmed tasks. It was an odd state to be in. It felt as though I was on the edge of my own existence, in some sort of transitional state between life and death.

I've experienced depression before, but this was something different. I was hollow, and the pain I felt from Jenna was my new baseline. I was a failure of a sister. I failed Jenna. I failed Mother Mary. I failed myself.

I wasn't worthy of being an older sister. I wasn't worthy of anything less than my new tortured baseline. A good sister would have been able to help. She would have saved Jenna from addiction and guided her through the darkness to a happy life.

The sleepless nights continued, as did my recurring nightmare of Jenna in the McDonald's bathroom, taunting me about what the future would bring now that I was a useless sister.

It echoed through me and found its way into every aspect of the day. Never allowing me to forget.

I tried attending a few Al-Anon meetings downtown, hoping I could find answers there. It's a support group for the family and friends of addicts. Surely, they would know what to do.

After going three or four times, I realized they had no answers for me. It was nothing more than a crying circle: cold, gray steel folding chairs aligned to face one another in a large, empty room.

Each person shared their pain, their story. One person would start to cry, which would trigger another to begin crying. The host of the group would offer comfort and a listening ear. I wasn't interested in sitting in a circle with strangers and crying. I needed resolutions, action, answers.

The frustration intensified and I felt alone. Did no one else feel like me? Was no one else searching for what I needed? Everywhere I turned, there were no answers. No one wanted to speak plainly and openly to me about this situation.

All I ever got were sad eyes and silence. I hated their sad eyes and their closed mouths. I desired directness and action. Why couldn't I find it? I was on a scavenger hunt to help Jenna, yet no one seemed able to give me even the smallest hint.

I tried looking things up online, but I never seemed to find anything there either. *"Have boundaries, stop enabling, practice self-care."* It all fell on deaf ears because none of it seemed applicable to my situation.

None of those things could help me with Jenna. I wasn't enabling her. I had set some boundaries. Self-care? Well, I couldn't even think about myself. I needed to help Jenna, not take a hot bath.

There's something about being an older sister. You feel obligated to care for the younger siblings. It's some sort of innate duty you are born with. I have always felt like this with Jenna.

I've always tried to fill in the gaps left by Mother Mary.

Though, sometimes I teetered between guiding Jenna and being alongside her.

When I got my very first apartment I used to have Jenna over on the weekends. I would buy vodka, rum and beer and always had plenty of marijuana to smoke. We would have some people over get drunk and party even though Jenna was underage.

One party in particular, I did a line of cocaine in the kitchen while Jenna sat in the living room. She saw me do it, but I was more concerned with tasting good cocaine for once. Jenna was offered some, but I rejected the opportunity for her.

There was another time, years later, that Jenna and I went to a bar to watch a band play. Someone drugged my drink, and I was nearly incapacitated.

I stumbled to the bathroom and then found myself outside on the ground surrounded by a couple of men. Jenna came outside, picked me up and dragged me into the car.

She drove us back to my apartment and put me to bed. The next morning, I realized what had happened. Two drinks would never get me buzzed let alone inebriated. I was too ashamed to admit that I had been drugged yet I was grateful that Jenna was with me. We never talked about it.

Getting drunk together, doing a line of cocaine in front of her, getting my drink spiked, were things that I regretted.

I often wondered if I contributed to her addiction in some way. If only she never saw me do anything. I would have been a better example to her. A wouldn't have come off as such a hypocrite.

I happened to fall asleep easily one night. It was a reprieve from the normal restlessness. Long after I had fallen asleep, the sound of my phone ringing startled me awake. I jumped out of bed and grabbed it, noticing the time was close to 1 AM.

It took a few moments to realize what was happening and whether I was asleep or awake. My heart was racing from the scare, and my eyes were hazy from exhaustion. I thought it could be a new nightmare, but it turned out to be otherwise.

As I reached for my phone to see who was calling, I saw that it was Jenna. Why was she calling me after midnight? I thought about answering it and then thought about healthy boundaries. I had to be awake early and felt that it was rude and inconsiderate of her.

I declined the call. After a moment, she called me again. I did the same thing, pushing her call to voicemail.

She then called me a third time. This time, I thought about my recurring nightmare. Was she dying and making one last call to me? Did she need help? I answered.

"Hello?" I cautiously asked with a voice shrouded in fear.

"Why didn't you answer my calls? Why did I have to call you so many times?" Jenna aggressively responded.

"What's going on? Is something wrong?" I asked, still half asleep.

"You should answer when I call you," Jenna demanded with a roughness in her voice.

"It's after midnight. I was asleep. Is something-" I again inquired with much less patience in my voice as Jenna cut me off.

"Yes, you need to answer my calls. I'm having a problem," she hissed.

She went on to tell me about a fight she just had with a guy she was dating. I was beyond pissed off. Why was she suddenly needing me for dating advice? She had never called me for something like this before.

I assumed there was no one else around for her to talk to, that I was her last option. Why would you call someone after midnight because you had a fight with your boyfriend? It was irrational, and she was frantic and distraught on the phone.

Sometimes we need people, I understand that. I wanted nothing more than to be there for her but not like this. She was demanding that I answer her calls at all hours of the night because she suddenly felt like using me as a punching bag.

I was very short with her and didn't want to get dragged into her drama or her dilemma. There was no calming her, so I got off the phone. My heart was racing as I lay in bed wide awake until the sun came up.

I was trying my best to navigate this, but I was lost and confused. It was becoming increasingly difficult to be connected to Jenna.

She has this way of making you disappear, of making you feel like you don't matter. She treats me similarly to how Cain treats her. I was petrified that she would overdose and die at any moment.

This left me feeling vulnerable and at her mercy. How was I supposed to balance boundaries with wanting to help her?

Deep inside, I felt like she knew she had power over me and my emotions. She knew that I was afraid of her dying. This was a tool for her to use to her advantage whenever she wanted.

It was manipulation at its peak. She was right; I was always afraid that she would die. That she would leave me. It left me open and vulnerable to her.

It meant that she could control me and my feelings. She could make me feel bad when she felt bad. She could make me feel powerless when she felt powerless. I was a pawn in her games, and we both knew it.

Most of that irrational behavior was due to her addiction, I knew that. Yet, I couldn't help but feel that she was the bad sister at times.

She was the one sucking others into her black hole of turmoil and suffering. That if we loved her, we should willingly come along for the ride. This phone conversation was a turning point for me.

There was a new guy at work. His name was Daniel. I really liked him in the sense that he was innocent. His youthful, chubby cheeks, thick black hair, kind eyes, and genuine personality drew me in immediately.

My favorite thing about him, though, was his laugh. It reminded me of the instant happiness you feel when you hear a baby laugh. It's purity and joy. His laugh brought me the same feelings.

I often requested to be in a section next to his, or I would sometimes switch with someone else so that I could be near him. I just wanted to hear every single laugh all night long.

I wanted to be in the presence of his innocence. It seemed to be bringing me back to life in odd ways, as though each laugh of his offered a spark of light in my dark state.

I couldn't help but love Daniel in the sweet way that you love a baby, a natural, automatic attraction to wholesomeness. A reminder that there was joy and light in the world.

One evening, Daniel and I were closing our sections and got to talking. We had exchanged pleasantries before, and we were always playful. Usually, our conversations were surface-level, exchanging pleasantries, jokes, smiles, or frustrations. Yet, this night was different.

I'm not sure how it even happened, but before I knew it, I had shared with him about Jenna, that my little sister was a heroin addict and that I was desperate to help her. That nothing I ever did worked and that she broke my heart over and over again.

Daniel listened until I was finished, then stopped what he was doing and walked up to me. Looking deep into my eyes, he shared that he, too, was a heroin addict. That he was sober for two months and living in transitional housing.

How could that be, though? He was sweet and innocent. He practically had a halo following him around. How could this beacon of light be an addict? It didn't make sense. To be honest, it's a truth that I still cannot believe to be legitimate.

Daniel went on to explain that there was nothing you could do for addicts. The desire and work to be sober must come from them. You can't force them to do anything. The more you try to demand change, the more they will retreat or dislike you.

Daniel went on to share that he also had an older sister who tried to help him in many ways, but he never cared about what she wanted or how she tried to help.

He looked at me with compassion and gently said, *"Nothing you do will get through to her. She will get sober if and when she wants to. Not when you want her to. I'm sorry."*

His words echoed throughout my entire body. I couldn't even absorb that he was an addict, let alone that my efforts for Jenna were futile.

Even though I was reeling from what just happened, a part of me felt comforted. I wasn't alone. I wasn't crazy. That small part of me loosened and relaxed for the first time in a long time.

I struggled with myself for the next several days. I was in a fog of bewilderment attempting to process everything Daniel had said.

How did this kind-hearted guy become an addict? I wanted to know every single detail, but it's inappropriate to inquire about things like that, especially with coworkers.

It didn't change how I felt or perceived him. Besides, I couldn't help but see his divinity. The light that he brought to every room he entered.

The laugh that made your heart melt. I still wanted to be within earshot of him at work. I still wanted to absorb every giggle he offered the world.

That being said, I needed to sit with myself on his advice regarding Jenna. He would know better than I. It took me a few weeks to clarify where I stood with Jenna and to consider what Daniel had told me. I sat down and wrote an email to Jenna:

Jenna,

I hope you have been doing well. I miss you, and Nashville just isn't the same without you. I'm not sure where you are or what you're doing, but I want you to know that I love you. You are my baby sister, and I would do anything for you. All I have ever wanted was for you to be healthy and happy. For you to find your way through the past and flourish into the future.

I have tried a lot of things to help you with your addiction, but it seems that nothing I do makes any difference. Nothing works. I don't know what I am doing, but I've tried my very best. I can't continue to participate in a relationship with you while you are actively addicted. It breaks my heart and causes me too much pain. This is something I have thought a lot about, hopefully you can see where I'm coming from.

I hope that you get the help that you seek and that you get better. I know that one day you and I will come back together and reconnect. We can restart as sisters and have a healthy, mature relationship. I love you with all my heart, and I hope that you reach back out to me once you are healthy and sober.

I will always love you and will always be   thinking of you.

Love, Amanda

I sent the email with a heavy heart. I knew it was the right thing to do, but I also felt like I was abandoning her in a time of need. I wrestled with the thought: how could I abandon her if she was rejecting me? What have I achieved through all my efforts?

I knew it needed to be done, but it hurt, and it wasn't easy. I was leaving her again. Just like I did when we were kids.

As a teenager, the torment from Mother Mary became unbearable, and I had a vision. I saw her killing me. In the vision, she stabbed me repeatedly with a kitchen knife.

I knew it was possible because, when she turned violent, her steel blue eyes went black, as though she were possessed. That dark side of her was undoubtedly capable of ghastly things.

Initially, the vision was from my own perspective. I lay on a bed, and Mother Mary approached me with her blackened eyes. She grinned, revealing her teeth as she raised the knife above me and stabbed me again and again, with an almost joyful intensity.

Then the vision became more vivid, I felt myself actually die. My soul lifted above my body, and I watched as she continued to stab me, even though I was already dead. There were moments when I thought it was about to happen in real life, so I prepared myself mentally and physically to die.

At sixteen, I had no choice but to leave her house. Either my vision would come true, and she would kill me, or I would end my own life from the torment she caused.

Either way, I would die. If I left, there was at least a chance of survival. However slim that chance was, it was better than staying.

Abandoning Jenna when we were children was heartbreaking, I don't think she ever forgave me. She always refused to talk about it. When I tried to push her to open up, she would close off entirely.

Jenna reminded me of myself during my forced therapy sessions as a child: slumped in a chair, arms crossed, eyes fixed on the floor, mentally disconnected. I wanted her to tell me if she understood why I left.

I wanted her to tell me if she hated me, if she felt abandoned. But we never had that conversation, she never allowed it. If she felt abandoned by me back then, I wondered if she felt the same way now. I certainly did.

I failed Jenna so many times, leaving her alone in moments of need again and again. Was I a monster? I felt like one. Yet, what more could I do? No, I tried. I had done what I could.

Jenna's response to my email was aggressive. She called me selfish, accused me of being dramatic, and said I was exaggerating. She asked, *"What kind of sister leaves?"*

It was a fair question, especially since this wasn't the first time I'd left her. Even though I was hurt by my decision it needed to be done.

It felt like all she wanted was for me to keep playing the role of a pawn in her games. I couldn't. I was too drained. I had nothing left to give her, no fight, no heart. My soul was ready to vacate.

I never responded to her email. I let it linger in the void. My heart ached with guilt and remorse. If only I had a solution for her.

If only I knew how to be a better sister. If only I hadn't left at sixteen. If only we'd had a loving home. If only every single thing had been different.

The pain of cutting myself out of Jenna's life weighed heavily on me. I felt like a disappointment, wandering through life like a zombie, detached from reality. I existed in a liminal space, where my body stayed on Earth, while my soul drifted aimlessly, longing for escape.

The only thing that made me feel alive was the gym. Slamming down on the treadmill at night, when the place was quiet, became my ritual.

It was the one outlet for all my frustration and stored energy. I pushed the treadmill to its limits, running so fast I nearly fell off. I wanted to be on the brink, on the edge of collapse, because I already felt dead inside.

Sometimes, the gym staff would check on me. I was friendly with them, and they knew I was dealing with family issues. To be honest, they might have been more concerned about the treadmill than me, afraid I'd break it.

Some nights, I'd talk about what was going on. Other nights, I'd wave them off to preserve my trance. As the days dredged on, I knew that something needed to change.

I needed to leave Nashville. It was time. I hated the weather, the traffic and the turmoil of Jenna's visits. Not to mention the torment of my own mind. I might not be able to escape my mind, but I could change my surroundings.

As I planned to leave, a co-worker at LongHorn told me about a tarot card reader that she recently visited. I decided to get a reading before I left town. I contacted the woman and made an appointment.

I arrived at her house as she kindly welcomed me in and guided me to the kitchen table. Her home was cluttered in a way that revealed decades of living and slow accumulation. The table looked out into the backyard. Vibrant colors and soft sounds from outside gently circled the room.

I had gotten readings before, and some were better than others. This was the first time that I got a reading from a normal deck of playing cards.

I wondered if they were just for show or if the three of clubs actually meant something. Toward the end of the reading, she said something. Well, she saw something.

"I see death. In less than two years," she softly conveyed as she searched my face for a reaction.

Using the palms of my hands I pushed myself away from the table in refusal of what she just said. My stomach dropped and my heart tingled. I felt dizzy and instantly thought of Jenna.

"Who? Don't tell me. Is it Jenna? My sister? Please tell me. No. No, don't tell me," I frantically replied as I teetered

between whether or not I wanted to know.

Anyone I knew could die and I would be fine. Except her. She can't die yet. We have to grow old together. We have to get wrinkled skin and weak bones at the same time. We have to take short strolls as we reminisce about our younger years.

The tarot reader saw my distressed reaction and looked as though she regretted saying it. She felt sorry for me and didn't want to agitate me further.

"No, it's not Jenna," she comforted.

My heart rate began to normalize. If it wasn't Jenna, then it was probably Mother Mary. I'd survive that. Yet, I was bothered by something.

It felt false. It felt as though she only said that to calm me and move on. Was Jenna going to die soon?

My mind swirled and even though there were fifteen minutes left to the reading, I couldn't hear anything else she said. My chest burned with her ominous premonition. My ears closed in an attempt to self-preserve.

The following few days blended and twisted. I was petrified about what the tarot reader told me, yet life dredged on. My lease came to an end as I packed up my short life in Nashville.

I had no idea where I wanted to go but I decided that going south to get away from the cold would be the best option. I still wanted to stay in the US because of Jenna but I needed to be close to the ocean.

I returned the furniture Isaac, and the other southern gentlemen had lent me, packed what I could, and donated the rest. Saying goodbye to them was hard.

I loved those men, they made me feel safe and never asked for anything in return. I promised to keep in touch, but I knew better. I knew I wouldn't.

Once again, I crammed my life into the trunk of my car and set off with no destination in mind. It was both liberating and terrifying to be a wanderer, a tumbleweed in the wind.

I wanted to be near the ocean and avoid snow, but that ruled out much of the map. And I had no interest in experiencing a natural disaster, so places like Texas, Florida, and the lower eastern coastline were out.

I swept through Mississippi, Alabama, and Georgia. I had never been to any of those states before, and I wanted to see what all the hillbilly jokes were based on.

Maybe I didn't spend enough time there, but I found life to be relaxing. It was simple, with a more country-style way of living. People didn't dress to impress, and they didn't seem to care much about how their houses looked, at least from the outside.

There were a few areas I drove through that felt like

they could swallow you whole. As though, if you went missing, no one would even come looking, let alone find you.

As a woman traveling alone, my fear instinct perked up a few times. To be honest, there are dark aspects of my inner self, and I found it oddly arousing to toy with the fantasy of disappearing.

I wasn't too far removed from vanishing as it was. The idea of going down in history as someone who just disappeared sounded like a fun way to be remembered.

Podcasts could be made about me, leaving people wondering for decades. There'd even be a cold case file about me, collecting dust in some storage facility.

When I reached Savannah, Georgia, I enjoyed the canopy trees draped over the roads. It was a beautiful place to explore. I thought about staying, but something nudged me to go to Florida. As a New Hampshire native, Florida was for the elderly, the retired, or those quirky people in Miami stuck in the '80s. Even though I had no reason to go, that tiny inner voice urged me.

Since I had no clear direction and plenty of time, I figured, why not? I made my way down the coast, exploring several parts of Florida.

I wasn't sure what I was looking for, but I trusted the process. Daytona led to Orlando, which brought me to Tampa. The beaches in St. Petersburg were stunning, and

Tampa felt relaxed.

I sat on a stone wall that lined the coast on Bayshore Boulevard in downtown Tampa. My feet dangled over the edge as the water splashed and swirled beneath them.

Unique birds soared overhead, hunting for lunch, while a refreshing breeze provided a sense of calm. *I like it here*, I thought. *It's nice. I think I could live here.*

I slept in my car for a few nights before booking an Airbnb for three nights. Was this where that tiny inner voice wanted me to be? How could I even tell?

That voice was faint, barely assertive. Sometimes I couldn't hear it at all. I decided to test it, make a deal with the Universe. I'd try for one apartment. If I got it, that would be my sign to stay. If not, I'd keep moving south.

That was exactly what I did. I went on Craigslist and casually searched for a room to rent. I wasn't serious about looking and only skimmed the first page of results.

One ad caught my eye: a college student trying to get out of her lease. The room was fully furnished and included a private bathroom.

I contacted her and arranged to see the apartment the following morning. She was nice, and the apartment was quiet. There were four rooms in total, each with a private bathroom.

All the tenants were college-aged women. Six

months remained on the lease, and she offered to cover the transfer fees. I agreed, and we walked to the leasing office together.

I filled out the application and left without any expectations. With no job and only a few references other than my apartment in Nashville and the waitressing job, that I quit.

I drove out of the apartment complex fully expecting to never hear from them again. Fully expecting to continue on my journey to find a destination.

Less than two hours later, my phone rang. The number was from Florida. I didn't know anyone in Florida, so I figured it was the Universe giving me a nudge.

When I answered, it was the leasing office. They had approved my application and asked me to come by to pay the deposit and sign the lease.

I was in utter disbelief as we got off the phone. No way. Did they really just approve someone without a job? Well, I'd made a deal with the Universe, so I guess Tampa was where I'd stay, at least for now.

I had to wait three weeks to move in, so I slept in my car and showered at Planet Fitness. Without a job, I needed to save every penny. The excitement of having a place kept me going through the uncomfortable nights, while my days were spent exploring Tampa, Clearwater, and St. Petersburg.

It was March so the weather was perfect. Being outside felt refreshing. For the first time in a long while, I felt happy and excited. Carefree. Unburdened. Like I had a fresh start. My steps were light and bounced with optimism.

Moving into the room was smooth. It came furnished with a bed, nightstand, dresser, desk, and TV. All utilities, including Wi-Fi, were included in the rent.

I didn't have a TV in Nashville, so this felt like a luxury. Most nights, I lounged in the queen-sized bed, watching TV until I drifted off to sleep.

The other women in the apartment seemed fine, but I kept my distance. With shared kitchen and living spaces, I avoided unnecessary interactions.

I figured it was better to lay low until I secured a job and income. After all, I was only here for six months and preferred peace.

I got a job delivering packages for Amazon. The work was straightforward and paid decently. Although the hours could be long and getting routes through the app wasn't always easy, it was a refreshing change from waitressing. It also gave me a chance to familiarize myself with Tampa and St. Petersburg.

With rent under $600 and all utilities included, I didn't need to work too much. This allowed me to explore hobbies and enjoy my new city.

I hired a personal boxing coach and trained three times a week. It helped me get into shape quickly and provided an outlet for my frustrations. Bit by bit, I was reclaiming life. Slowly, I began to feel alive again.

CHAPTER TWELVE

∴

"Sometimes, when you're in a dark place, you think you've been buried, but you've actually been planted."

Christine Caine

Life in Tampa was going well. I felt relaxed and rejuvenated. Perhaps it was the new city, the new state, or the excitement of getting acquainted. I thought less about Jenna and more about myself. I was making myself happy again.

I had freed myself from the chains of Jenna, the chains of expectation, forcefulness, fantasy, responsibility, and accountability. I allowed Jenna to continue living the same life she had led for over a decade. Her life was her decision. My life was mine.

I was open to helping Jenna if I genuinely thought she wanted help, but I wasn't interested in detoxing with her for a third time.

I had released myself from the shadow of Jenna. I no longer wanted to reside there, and I had decided I would no longer participate in her self-inflicted destruction. If Jenna wanted something different, she would have to help herself. I was at peace with that. I was at ease.

Conversations with Mother Mary had all but stopped. She liked to remind me of my decision to separate from Jenna, often attempting to make me feel bad or guilty about it. As a mother of two children, she did an excellent job of pretending there was only one.

I was tired of her psychological manipulation. Always trying to make me the bad guy so that she isn't. After a while, it really starts to wear you down, but I wasn't about to allow anyone to belittle me.

I had suffered immensely for Jenna. I had sacrificed and continued to sacrifice for her. I had done my part. I deserved to live my life.

Being in Tampa allowed me to restart a life in the US on my own terms. I could live where I wanted and spend my days how I liked. I quickly made several new friends and began going out for lunch, dinner, and sightseeing. I even went on a few dates.

I was laughing again. I felt revived. It felt good to focus solely on myself again. I cared only about what brought me joy, and I was happy to be in that state of mind.

I received a message from a former coworker at LongHorn, in Nashville. She and I had never spoken much, so her message intrigued me. Sadly, Daniel had died from an overdose. They had started dating shortly after I left Nashville.

She explained that she wasn't sure what my relationship with Daniel had been but mentioned that he liked me and spoke highly of me. She asked if I would write a letter to his family.

I reread her message several times. My heart broke for Daniel and his family. Tears slid down my cheeks as I thought about the light he brought into the world, his glorious giggle and a smile that shone like a halo.

He was too extraordinary for this world, yet too extraordinary to leave it. My heart felt heavy as I sat in dismay, pondering his plight. How could such a beautiful soul be so deeply intertwined with darkness? It wasn't fair, not to him, not to the world.

Daniel was alluring in a way I had never experienced before; he was radiant, and I hated that he walked with darkness. How could both dualities coexist so strongly within one person? He hid his darkness masterfully. To look at him, you would never know anything other than light.

Daniel gave me the greatest gift anyone could have given me: freedom from my misery with Jenna. He handed me the key to resolve, simply by offering words rather than sad eyes.

He enlightened me about addiction and the helplessness surrounding it. He made me feel normal and unashamed.

After taking a day to process, I sat down and wrote a letter to Daniel's family. I wept for his parents and sister. I considered if Daniel even saw his own greatness or realized how special he was. I could never forget what he did for me; the kindness and openness he showed me that night at the restaurant.

I hoped that his family could find some comfort in the impact that Daniel had on me. How I saw his light and valued his presence in the world. No matter what he struggled with, he was a good person who impacted everyone around him. Daniel will forever have a place in my heart.

After writing the letter to his family, I sent it to Daniel's girlfriend. I reflected on the pain his family must feel. I couldn't help but tie it into my own experience with Jenna. Would I too know their pain one day? That sentiment lingered in the background of my new life.

As time continued, I settled into Tampa and my

thoughts of India faded. I no longer mourned India or Hampi. I stopped calling the village and Akash, stopped sending money, and tried to move on with my life.

The village had an immense impact on me. Its pull was magnetic, and I couldn't maintain a life in Tampa while still connected to it.

I sometimes caught myself wondering if I would ever find the love and connection that I felt in Hampi. Would I ever feel that way about a group of people or a place again? While I enjoyed Tampa, the connection wasn't the same.

Perhaps I needed to accept that maybe nothing ever would be. Maybe that was my only taste of true love and family. Maybe my gift was a moment, not a lifetime. I had no choice but to accept that possibility.

Though a small part of me still aspired to return someday, I had to keep that dream in the background. I couldn't function with sadness at the forefront.

It was true that my heart remained with India, but my mind needed to be in Florida. The love I held for India would never waver, but I could still live my life, regardless of location.

One afternoon, I received a Facebook message from Jenna. She said she was in Florida and that she was doing well. She didn't ask how I was doing. She didn't say she missed me or loved me. It was just a message saying she was in Florida.

I clenched my jaw and tightened my lips. Really? She couldn't even ask how I was doing? Not even a superficial, *"Hope you're well"*? It was all about her. As always, nothing about me whatsoever.

After everything, all these years, battles, and sacrifices, and she couldn't even offer a polite greeting? I deleted the message without responding. Did she even like me? Did she care about me at all? Was I just a pawn, a resource she turned to in desperation?

Anger bubbled inside me. I wanted to both cry and punch a hole in the wall. Fuck her and her selfishness. I wanted to be validated. I wanted someone, anyone to acknowledge what I did for Jenna. What I continued to do for her.

The life I gave up for her and the life I now had because of her. I guess I really was an only child, a detached piece of lineage, forgotten and discarded.

Mother Mary and I continued not to speak. She was still angry that I had cut off contact with Jenna. According to her I was wrong, that I was abandoning Jenna in her time of need.

Apparently, we were all supposed to sacrifice everything for Jenna, the beloved Jenna. We were expected to bow at her feet. We were supposed to drown alongside her.

When I was about eighteen or nineteen, I went to see my doctor to get a yearly check-up. I went to the same doctor that Jenna and I had been going to, off and on, since we were kids.

At the end of the check-up the doctor said something that shocked me. Shocked and infuriated me is more accurate. With my mouth open, she shined a light to check my throat.

As she looked, she started to confess something. A secret that she had been holding onto for many years, and it finally forced its way to the surface.

"I know about you and your sister. I know you were being abused," she casually admitted as she turned away to grab something from the counter behind her.

While still turned away from me, she continued to speak, *"What was I supposed to do? If I reported it, they would have taken you away. You probably would have gotten separated, and your life would have been worse. You wouldn't have wanted that, would you?"*

I was too stunned to respond. She knew we were being abused, and she did nothing? How could she have possibly made that decision? She knew what was best for two innocent children who were abused? How would she even know how bad it was to decide that?

My mind turned to mush as I attempted to

conceptualize what she just said. Not only the ethics behind it but why she suddenly needed to confess this to me.

I didn't need her to validate my childhood. Yet, she could have saved us and didn't bother. She decided to do what doctors do best and play God.

I struggle with this information to this day. I wonder how different life would have been for Jenna and me. Even if we had gotten separated, life could have been better.

Maybe Jenna would have never been an addict. Maybe I would have been loved. Sure, it could have been worse, but it could have also been much better.

Even though Mother Mary is attempting to make me feel badly for everything that's happened with Jenna, it's odd that she never seems to acknowledge that the entire reason for this suffering is because of her.

She's shifting the blame so that I'm the bad one. I'm the failure. I'm the one who must pay for her mistakes. I was defiant as a child, and I remain defiant as an adult.

I refuse to be dragged down with Jenna. I refuse to have my experience minimized. I will not be a figure in the shadows.

It took me years of therapy and a lot of self-development to overcome my childhood. I did the work to elevate and heal. Though there are parts of me that are shattered, missing or duct-taped, I did the work.

I never ran away and evaporated into drugs. I never asked others to sacrifice anything for me. I never forced my lifestyle onto others. The audacity of people to ask that of me was beyond infuriating.

Come to think about it, being a tumbleweed in the wind wasn't that bad after all. At least the tumbleweed is disconnected and free.

After my six-month lease had ended, I moved into a two-bedroom house by myself. I have never rented a house on my own before.

I was happy to live alone again and excited to try something different. I had a driveway, a yard, neighbors, and more importantly, peace.

Since I went from a fully furnished room to a two-bedroom house, I had no furniture. No bed or anything else for that matter. I jumped online and quickly found a used mattress for sale.

I had the seller help put it on the roof of my Honda Civic. I strapped it on and made the journey home. It was heavy bringing it into the house alone, but I did it. I had somewhere to sleep.

I befriended one of the maintenance guys at the old apartment complex. He gave me some used furniture from the complex that was going to be thrown out. I was grateful that he gave me a dresser, side table, TV stand, kitchen table, and lounge chair.

Apartment buildings are always noisy, and you can hear your neighbors every move. From walking upstairs and having sex to fighting and playing instruments. In a house, you hear none of that. I reveled in a new level of tranquility.

I once lived in an apartment in New Hampshire where the walls were paper thin. I could hear my neighbors talking at a normal volume.

When they had sex, it sounded like it was in my apartment. I hated bringing anyone over because I never knew what sounds would come through the walls.

If a female friend was over, we would laugh about it. If a potential love interest was over, it was awkward. I only stayed in that place for one year because of it. Now, I could freely listen to music or turn the TV volume up without a care in the world.

I swapped the Amazon delivery job for pet sitting which started out slow but quickly expanded. I could host pets in my house without having to worry about neighbors or management.

I had a fence installed in my backyard which allowed me to take groups of dogs at a time without worrying about walking the whole pack together. I was building a great clientele and learning a lot about pets and people too.

A lot of mistakes were made at the beginning, but I learned and adapted quickly. I had much more freedom as a pet sitter. I could hang out at home with the dogs and make money.

I could be at my client's houses and watch Netflix while getting paid. I could take dogs for walks and get paid. Once I got the hang of it and established a system, it was easy and relaxing. Far better than driving the streets delivering packages for Amazon.

While hosting a dog at my house, we went out for our morning walk. I usually go in the same direction every day. Today, my tiny inner voice told me to walk in the opposite direction. I listened.

We walked for about ten or fifteen minutes when I happened to look off to the right-hand side and saw a pit bull laying in the grass. It was a larger sized dog that was obviously dead. I jumped back in shock.

I've never come across a dead dog before and having him laying outside just off the sidewalk scared me. Once we got back home, I called animal control and told them where the dog was located so they could go and collect it.

A few hours later, I got a text from Jenna's cousin, Hannah. She asked if I was available to talk on the phone. I was excited, I love Hannah. She's such a sweet young lady.

I connect with her because she's had a very difficult

life and is trying to navigate an existence beyond it. As soon as I saw her text, I called her.

"Hey girl! How are you? What are you up to?" I asked with an eagerness to hear her voice.

"Where are you?" Hannah inquired.

"At home. Why? What's up?" I asked, leaning back in my chair.

"I have to tell you something," she expressed in a sunken tone.

"Tell me, girl. Anything," I responded.

"Jenna died this morning. Cain found her at a motel," she revealed.

"What?! No! What do you mean? Are you sure?" I implored. My body felt a rush of cold and tingled with fear. My deepest fear was coming true. My ears buzzed as I attempted to choked back tears.

"Yes. I'm so sorry, Amanda," she expressed.

"How did she die? What happened? Was she alone?" I frantically questioned. My throat was beginning to close as I attempted to ask before it was too late.

"They'll have to do tests, but they think it was an overdose," Hannah affirmed.

I burst into tears and then quickly collected myself. The room was spinning, or perhaps I was. Either way, I felt like I was in a time warp. I got off the phone and quickly called

Cain. He picked up after a few rings.

"*Is it true? Is it true? Is it true? Cain, is it true? Is it true? Is it true? Is it true? Is it TRUE?!*" I repeatedly asked in a heightened state of panic.

I was stuck. The only thing I could say was, "*Is it true?*" I felt like a record scratching over and over, unable to move forward. No other words formed. Nothing else would escape my mouth.

They were the only words my brain would allow. I desperately wanted him to say no; to tell me it was a joke or that Jenna was alive but in the hospital. I wanted him to tell me it was a lie, that Hannah was mistaken.

He finally broke and said, "*Yes, I'm sorry. It's true. It's true. I'm so sorry, baby. She's gone. Her skin was so cold.*"

I burst out into a cry that was half-muffled, half-infantile. This couldn't be, though. It couldn't be. Not my sweet, innocent Jenna. Gone? No, it couldn't be. No!

He was distressed and could hardly form a few sentences between his cries. Cain was the second youngest of eight children.

He had already experienced the death of several siblings, some of whom he had found himself. I could only imagine how much it would hurt to find your only child, dead. Alone. Cold in a motel room.

I got off the phone with Cain and had to call Mother

Mary. No one had notified her yet, and that was going to have to be my task. We hadn't spoken in at least a year.

Now, I had to tell her that her baby was dead. I called her several times, but she didn't answer. I suppose she didn't want to talk to me. She had no idea what was about to happen to her world.

I composed myself and left a voicemail before calling her father, my grandfather. I asked if I had her correct phone number and informed him that it was urgent. I then had to tell him that his grandchild was found overdosed that morning.

We both wailed on the phone. My stomach churned, and I felt nauseous. I needed to throw up. I couldn't handle this. I didn't want any of this.
This can't be happening right now. I must be dreaming.

I rubbed my eyes and shook my shoulders, hoping to wake up, hoping it was just a bad dream. It wasn't. This was real. This was my life.

I hung up with him and tried Mother Mary again. This time she answered. She sounded annoyed that I was calling and not happy to speak with me.

"Where are you?" I asked in my best attempt at a normal voice.

"Why?" Mother Mary questioned.

"Please, just tell me. Where are you? Are you at home?" I pressed with urgency. My composure was about to crumble as I was no longer able to hold back the tsunami of emotions.

She was hesitant and didn't want to answer. The words barely left her lips and sounded like they escaped without permission.

"Yes, why Amanda. What do you want? What is it?" she said in an annoyed tone.

"Jenna died," I blurted out with both relief and remorse.

"What?!" she exclaimed.

"I'm so sorry. I'm so sorry Mom," I conceded as a flood of tears rushed down my face.

"No!" she refused.

"Cain found her this morning at a motel. She was already gone when he arrived. I'm so sorry," I expressed.

In that instant, she wailed. It reminded me of the wail she released the night she found out that Jenna was using heroin. It was primal, animal. A wail that only a mother can make. We stayed on the phone for only a few more seconds after that. She said that she had to get off the phone.

The call disconnected and I was left sitting at my

kitchen table in utter disbelief. My whole body froze and my hearing faded. I was in shock. I was all alone. I was going to be sick.

I ran to the bathroom and dry heaved as my body shook and convulsed. Once I finished, I fell to the floor in the hallway, unable to breathe. My body was overcome with a level of sorrow I had never known before. I wailed and wailed until it brought me pain.

My mind was rejecting the reality that Jenna was gone. It was too monumental to be real. It was impossible for this to be real.

She's everything to me. She's the only person on Earth that I love. It's impossible that I no longer love anyone on this Earth.

Collapsed on the floor I continued to cry like a starving infant. I sobbed and screamed. I pleaded to the powers of the Universe for this to not be real.

I begged for it to not be real. I continued to cry until I ran out of energy. Until I nearly passed out from exhaustion.

Like a sick child I wanted Mother Mary. I wanted her to comfort me, to relieve the pain. In my mind, there was no one else to call.

As that wasn't an option, I remained alone with the physical and emotional ache of losing Jenna. Attempting to accept the reality that I staunchly rejected.

That night was agonizingly painful and consisted of tears, haunting thoughts and a failed attempt at bargaining. I tried to exchange my life for hers.

She deserved it more than me. If someone had to die, I would rather it be me. Sleep wasn't an option as my entire world came to a screeching halt.

We made her arrangements on the phone the following day. Deciding to cremate her, choosing how her service would go, what her obituary would say, and which flowers to purchase. Mother Mary was on the call as well and she and Cain bantered about how to spell Jenna's middle name.

It was an exchange that had occurred since we were children. Cain and Mother Mary arguing about whether her middle name was spelt with an *"e"* or an *"a"*. Jenna couldn't settle the debate when she was young.

However, once she was older, they would always ask her to spell her middle name. It didn't matter how many times Jenna had told them; they would need her to settle it again in a future argument.

Here on the phone, making Jenna's arrangements, there was no one to confirm which letter it was. Neither of them knew and it was still a mystery. Eventually, they came to an agreement on which letter to use for the final time.

It felt surreal. It had to be a new nightmare. I desperately wanted it to be. I tried my best to disconnect from reality so that I could make it through.

Cain's second family were also on the phone chiming in. I hated them just as much as I hated Cain. They were part of Jenna's downfall. They participated, stroked the flames, and sabotaged Jenna.

Hearing them attempt to have any input on my sister's arrangements infuriated me. She was my sister, not theirs. They wanted her to fail, and their wishes were fulfilled. I didn't want to give them the satisfaction of choosing anything for the conclusion of Jenna's life.

We decided to have Jenna embalmed so that I would have enough time to return to New Hampshire. Having the extra time was a relief. It allowed me the space to also process what was happening.

Funeral services always seem rushed. The day someone dies is the same day that their arrangements are made. It blurs and feels like an aggregated mass of time comprised of delirium and motion.

It was winter and here I was again in New Hampshire. Jenna always seems to bring me here when it's freezing cold. She must be doing it on purpose. Laughing at me from above and forcing memories of our childhood to flood my mind.

When we were in elementary school, Jenna and I went for a ski trip during the winter holiday break. Well, she chose to snowboard, and I skied.

The school bussed us to the mountain, and we spent hours going up and down the trails. Meeting at the chairlift to ride back up and exchange stories.

Her fearless endeavors on the black diamond slopes forced me to level up and join her. Life was always so much more exciting with Jenna next to me.

Her wildness wrapped around me and lassoed me in like a cow in Texas. I was eager to join her as I always felt safe.

Before leaving Florida to go up north, I went to Goodwill to buy a winter jacket. I found the funniest shirt possible for Jenna's services.

It was a button-up dress shirt with white and red stripes. The back of the shirt and sleeve cuffs were lined with small red pom-pom balls.

Jenna would have either been completely embarrassed by it or thought it was the funniest shirt in the world. Either way, it would have been a perfect response. Either way, she would be smiling down on me.

Arriving at the funeral home left me with an upset stomach and a tightness in my chest. The majority of me was in denial. I didn't want her to be gone. I didn't want to know life without her wildness beside me.

How is someone here one moment and completely gone the next? It's just not possible. My brain couldn't compute so it was shifting my reality to cope and preserve.

Upon entering the building, I asked someone to guide me away from Jenna. I blocked my peripheral view and walked to the back area sitting room.

I stayed there until the very end of the service doing my best to remain calm. Though I didn't want to face it, it was time.

Mother Mary and another person escorted me up to view Jenna. It was the worst sight I have ever seen. I collapsed in front of her and unsuccessfully choked back infant cries. It was just her shell. The remnants of what used to be. Her essence was no longer here.

I played with her long dark hair just as we used to do when we were children. When we would comfort each other late at night. Now it was my turn to comfort her. Even if it's just her shell that I was touching.

It was real. It was right in front of my face. Yet, I still didn't want to believe it. I wanted this to be the world's most horrific joke. For her to rise up, point at me, smirk and say, *"Gotcha!"*

I wanted it not to be true. This must be a dream, right? Please. I rubbed my eyes and shook my shoulders.

Nope, this is not a dream. This is my life. It was hard to leave Jenna's side. They kept asking me to leave her since the services were ending.

How could I leave her side though? How could you ask me to leave my sweet, innocent baby Jenna behind. How is she supposed to be alone in this dark and musty building? Who will keep her company? Who will hold her hand?

She needs someone. I have to abandon her again? She'll never forgive me if I do. I'll never forgive myself if I do.

After some convincing, I stood up and walked away from her. This would be the very last moment that her physical form is here on Earth, is seen.

Walking away from her meant that I would never see her beautiful full lips, long hair, tooth gap, sparkling eyes, or her beauty mark ever again.

My stomach twisted in my body with the reality of this. It really was the end for us. Except, she was the one who left me this time.

The following day was her wake. She was cremated and placed in a beautiful glass urn with two monarch butterflies on it. This day was easier to manage since her body was gone.

The hardest part for me was the visitors.

The fellow heroin addicts. The dealers. The connections. The anger that I felt boiled at the surface of my skin. I wanted every one of those fuckers to get burned alive.

I wanted to be the one to light them on fire. I wanted to make them all feel my pain. They contributed to Jenna's death, and I hated them for it.

Cain was holding it together as much as expected. He looked as though a sudden breeze would dismember him. I kept my eye on him to make sure he was around people and keeping his composure.

Mother Mary was stoic and didn't stay long. She brought her latest boyfriend and kept her distance. Mother Mary sure can catch a man. She has always gone from one man to another my entire life. They would often overlap as well.

She's always been very beautiful and knows how to work her assets. I'm not sure what kind of spell you would need to cast on a man for him to be in the next room while you abuse your child. She knows the one though.

I remember once when Jenna and I were children, she got engaged to a man that we had never even met. I hated all the men. All the moving. All the fallouts.

Perhaps that's why I swung in the opposite direction. My only goal in life has always been to be nothing like her.

Dating habits were no exception.

I'm sure she needed her latest boyfriend for support. She probably would feel like a loser if she showed up to her daughter's funeral without a companion. Even though we have a sorted past, I needed Mother Mary more than anyone else. I needed her to support me.

I wanted us to support each other. I was falling apart and no one understood. I needed a familiar person, one who also knew Jenna like I did. Naturally, Mother Mary wasn't interested in being there for me. She only worried about herself and her latest companion.

Mother Mary even found a way to make me feel worse at Jenna's service. She reminded me that I chose not to have a relationship with Jenna. That I chose not to talk to her and that I was now facing the guilt and consequences of that.

When you think you can't feel any worse, Satan will find a way. I hated her for saying that to me at my sister's funeral. What a bitch. What an absolute bitch.

In my life, I have often felt bad for Mother Mary. Sometimes making excuses for her. This is what had always led me to reestablishing communication with her.

It's not long before she ultimately reveals her true self, and I remember why I don't speak with her to begin with. I remember why I hate her.

The comments she made at Jenna's service solidified it for me. The coldness, the intentional infliction of distress, the dismissiveness. What kind of mother would say that? I could never feel bad for her ever again. Not after this.

I stayed in New Hampshire for several days following Jenna's services. The funeral home split her ashes into thirds. One-third for Cain, one-third for Mother Mary, and one-third for me.

One-third turned out to be a bigger volume than I expected. They put the ashes in a thick plastic bag, closed it with a metal tie and placed it in a generic black plastic container.

That was all that I had left. Some ashes in a plastic container. As far as the world is concerned, she no longer exists. Do our memories also no longer exist? Has she been removed from Earth's directory?

Holding the container in my hands as I pondered the purpose of life. The funeral director was speaking to me, but his voice faded into the background.

We had her fingerprints taken before they cremated her. They were kept on file at the funeral home and were accessible by request.

I picked mine up the same day I received her ashes. Smeared black blots of ink on cream paper. Anguish vibrated through my body as I stared at them.

The funeral director continued saying something, but I couldn't hear him. Reality seemed to taper off and I was outside of the funnel. My body felt like it was swaying.

I couldn't be sure if it was me or my world. There was a buzz in my head which progressed into the sound of a heart monitor flatlining.

I left the funeral home with my head hung in disbelief. As I exited the building, the sounds of life around me, muffled. I couldn't hear what anyone was saying.

Words reverberated and echoed before they could reach me. By the time they did, it was indistinguishable.

The final task left was to go through Jenna's bedroom. I was shocked to see how clean it was. It was suspiciously clean. There was just no way you could convince me that she left her room in a militant style with not one thing out of place.

Cain and his second family must have already done a sweep. They must have hidden any evidence or taken anything valuable.

She was at the motel because she got kicked out of Cain's house. Yet, her room looked immaculate. I'm not a detective. I'm not even a decent kidnapper but this was obvious.

Being in her room made me feel cold and haunted. She didn't have very many things. She had a few clothing essentials hung up and folded. She had her makeup and other beauty products in a desk drawer.

There were stacks of paper on a table and her bed was neatly made. I went through every inch of her room even lifting the mattress. A drug addict with no paraphernalia? This room had been cleaned.

I sat in the chair where she would do her make-up. I looked through the drawer and imagined I was her for a moment.

Gently touching the products and inspecting what she liked to use. Holding them in my hand, I tried to see if her essence would communicate with me.

I wondered if holding them would bring me closer to her. If it would open some kind of portal so we could see each other for just a moment. I sat waiting, wishing, praying. It didn't.

I moved to the stack of paperwork. Most of it consisted of legal documents and papers from her childhood school days. It seemed odd that such different types of papers were grouped together. I wondered what Cain and his second family had removed from her room. I hated them all.

I started with the tall stack of legal documents. I glanced at her name printed in black ink. At least the middle name debate was finally settled. Here it was, in bold font. They agreed on the correct spelling after all.

To my shock, there were several cases against her. Jenna had been in and out of the legal system. She had actually gone to jail for over six months. When I read that, I had to pause. Jenna went to jail? When?

Jenna had been jailed for selling fentanyl to a woman who later overdosed and died. The police had already been surveilling Jenna and caught her selling to the individual who overdosed.

I matched the dates on the court documents to my own timeline with Jenna—the last time she came to Nashville to detox.

That time when she was so insistent about leaving immediately, it was because the cops were closing in on her after that woman's death. She thought she could get out of town for a while until things blew over.

Since she returned to New Hampshire after five or six weeks, it was clear she wasn't really on the run. She just used me. She played me.

She said all the magical words to make me agree to host her again, under the guise of wanting to get clean and change her life. In reality, she just needed a place to hide for a while.

What was real? Did she ever genuinely want help? Did she ever really want to get clean? My mind raced, dissecting every conversation, every sliver of hope she gave me. Was it all a practical joke? Was Amanda the fool she could play like a fiddle?

I felt like one. I felt ignorant for hoping she had a chance to get sober and change her life. For all the sleepless nights and long days that I spent fearing for her survival. I tormented myself in vain.

The legal documents illuminated just how much Cain had hidden. He ensured all her secrets were kept, guaranteeing her life would never change.

His words claimed he wanted her to get help, but his actions said otherwise. I watched that man cry in front of me, distressed over Jenna's addiction. Now that some of their secrets are revealed, I realize it was all a farce. He helped keep her addicted.

Not only had Jenna had been in trouble with the law multiple times, she also crashed several cars. Why did Cain keep providing her with cars when he knew she was using heroin and getting into accidents? The lack of accountability and awareness was utterly shocking.

Did he want her to kill herself? Or, worse, did he want her to kill an innocent person? How some people sleep at night is beyond my comprehension.

I remember while I was living overseas, Mother Mary called me and asked if Jenna could use my car until I returned to the US. I was beyond irate that she had the audacity to ask me to do something like that. Why would I ever give Jenna my car?

The car I worked so hard for? The car that I earned? To hand it over to someone who never accomplished anything, who never even tried? Of course, I rejected her request, but my annoyance at the situation fell on deaf ears.

Everyone wanted Jenna to have life served on a silver platter. We were all expected to pool our resources so she could remain a societal failure. That lack of responsibility was part of what turned Jenna into the tyrant she became. An entitled woman who preferred manipulation to achievement. I blame Cain and Mother Mary for their utter failure.

While going through Jenna's belongings, I took a few items, including a couple of rings from a small box. While I was living in Nashville, I took a three-month painting class.

For one of the assignments, I painted a tree in a field. I was pleased with how it turned out, using various shades of brown to give the trunk dimension and texture.

When I finished, I sent Jenna a photo, asking for her opinion. She told me it needed a tree swing. I never would have thought of that, but I loved the idea. I added one and sent her another photo to confirm it was complete. She said she liked it.

After the class ended, I sent her the painting as a gift.

Now, standing in her room, I wondered what had happened to it. It was gone. Did she even like it? Had she thrown it away immediately, or let it collect dust before discarding it? I would have loved to take it back to Florida.

I was plagued by the question as to whether or not our love, our relationship, had been a façade. Had I created a world to make myself feel better? Was it always one-sided or had we progressively lost each other?

We'd been distant since I left home at sixteen, but I'd always extended offers to her, opportunities to be with me. If I'm honest, she never put much effort into our relationship after I left. She never showed me much support, care, or love.

I guess I really was in a one-sided relationship. I wanted her far more than she ever wanted me. I loved her beyond comprehension, but she never loved me like that. Realizing this only broke my heart further.

I have a history of forcing myself onto others, of loving too quickly and making relationships into more than they are.

I shower people with my love, attention, and gifts. Maybe they think I'm desperate, but I'm not. I just crave deep love, a love I've never known.

I thought I had that love with Jenna. But now, nothing felt real. I cried in Jenna's room a few times and spent a night or two in her bed. Other than that, I avoided her room.

It had a bad energy. It felt cold, damp, and eerie, as

though chaos and fear lingered in the air. It gave me the chills.

Regardless, when I forced myself to stay in her room, it was in hopes that her spirit might visit me. That she'd reveal herself somehow.

Maybe make something fall. I sat on her bed hoping and wishing in vain. Nothing fell. She never appeared.

Perhaps I was in denial, unable to process the loss. Maybe that disqualified me from receiving visits from spirits. Or maybe she was already busy with her next life.

CHAPTER THIRTEEN

∴

*"The courage it took to get out of bed each morning to face
the same things over and over was enormous."*

Charles Bukowski

New Hampshire was cold, and there was snow on the
ground. It was nothing more than a reminder of
how much I hate the cold and snow. It's fun when you are a
child but a chore when you are an adult.

Wearing three pairs of socks didn't seem to keep my
feet warm, either. Florida has a reputation for being for
retirees, rednecks, and wannabe drug lords, but at least you
can wear sandals in January.

I tried not to complain but swallowing my gripes
turned out to be more difficult than I expected. I
compromised by complaining out loud to myself when I was
alone. At least my own ears heard the suffering.

I was able to meetup with a few old friends, which was a welcomed distraction. It was an escape from the reality of Cain's house and the death of Jenna. I acted as normal as possible. Well, it felt like I was acting normal, anyway.

We spent lots of time giggling and recalling moments from the past. It felt refreshing to at least smile and laugh even though I was dead inside. Everyone seemed to be doing well, and I was happy to see them, even if it was in bad circumstances.

After a week in New Hampshire, I was ready to leave. However, I was nervous about Cain's state of mind. I assumed that he would kill himself.   Actually, I was sure of it. How could a person live with themselves after all that anyway? Even though there really wasn't much that I could do for him I still worried.

I did blame Cain for the majority of Jenna's drug usage and death, but I never once shared that with him. I figured it might be the one thing that pushed him over the edge. I really didn't care what happened to him, but I wasn't going to be the one to bring him to his limit.

Containing my utter disdain for Cain was a challenge. Every cell in my body wanted to either watch or participate in a level of torture that would make the devil proud. His actions took

my sweet, innocent baby Jenna away from me. He's

responsible for my grief. He helped Jenna die.

That's the route that Cain chose, enabling. He would have rather maintained a dysfunctional relationship with Jenna. He wanted her to stay sick so that his world could continue to function as he preferred.

That's exactly what he did for over a decade. He slowly aided Jenna in her downward spiral and continued to refuse to help her in healthy ways. No matter what his mouth said, he wanted her to die.

His actions confirmed this. Or, at the very least, Jenna wasn't worth enough for Cain to change how he lived. He refused to allow Jenna to exit his black hole. Jenna played a role in his dysfunction, and he wasn't ever going to allow her to stop.

He had always functioned like that, though. After his separation from Mother Mary, he began dating an alcoholic with three children. She was a violent and sloppy drunk that couldn't be controlled.

She and Cain would often get into physical altercations that resulted in injuries, broken objects and sometimes the police.

She once attacked me while I was laying on the floor in the living room. She was drunk, as usual, and walked over to me and kicked the underside of my chin. It caused my head to get thrown back, and before I knew what was going on, she was on top of me, punching and attempting to restrain me.

My body immediately went into an anxiety attack as I fought for my life. After escaping, I ran to the neighbor's house, and they called the police. I had scratch marks, bruises and an injury to my tongue from the attack.

Cain never cared about what happened. It wasn't the first time she had attacked Jenna or me, nor was it the last. He's still with her to this day, and to this day, she's still an alcoholic.

The truth was that I didn't want Cain to die yet. I wanted him to live for a long time and suffer just like I was suffering. I wanted his heart to break, nights to be sleepless and torment to be ceaselessly haunting.

Making my way through the airport and back to Florida, I keep Jenna's ashes close to me at all times. I had put her box in a small backpack which was opened and examined by the TSA.

They asked what was in the box and I told them that it was my sister. The two agents looked at me solemnly. There are those sad eyes again. People love to give you sad eyes but not to give you words.

After they handed her back to me, I walked with the backpack clutched to my chest. Making my way to the gate and sitting in contemplation. My sister was in my arms. I was now tasked with carrying her with me for the rest of my life. I had to guard her and keep her safe.

Returning to Florida allowed me to detach from New Hampshire and all the old turmoil that rose to the surface while I was there. Once you escape torture, you never want to revisit ground zero. With Jenna, I've had to revisit it several times and I hope to never return.

As much as I wanted to get out of New Hampshire, being back in Florida meant one thing. It meant that I was now alone. There was no one around me. No one to distract me. No one to confide in.

When I was about seven or eight years old, all four of us went for a hike at a local mountain. Cain and Mother Mary were still married.

We lost track of time at the peak, and wound up getting lost after dark. It was terrifying. I remember walking along the trail, not being able to see anything from the blackness.

We walked in a single-file line. Cain was in front followed by Jenna, then Mother Mary and I was last. I tried holding onto Mother Mary's shirt because I was afraid I would get grabbed by an animal.

She angrily scoffed at me for touching her and I instantly let go. *Why was I behind them? Why was Jenna sandwiched between the comfort of two adults? I wanted to be protected. Why couldn't I be?* My little heart raced in my chest as I wondered something else.

What would happen if I just stayed on the mountain? Would they even care? Would they notice? I stopped walking to test my suspicion.

Standing on the dirt path I watched as all three of them carried on without ever looking back to see if I was still with them. Their figures slowly disappeared into the abyss.

I thought that it would be better if they left me. That perhaps I wasn't welcome or loved like Jenna. They would be happier without me.

I then wondered where I would sleep and what I would eat. I looked around trying to see something, anything. The sound of fallen tree limbs snapping echoed behind me.

A shiver swept through my body and I ran ahead to meet Mother Mary. I was too weak to be alone. *They would have to tolerate me until I was stronger,* I thought.

Back in Florida, I was left all alone with a new torment. The torment of grief. I've known people who have died. There were plenty. However, none of those people were as close to me as Jenna.

Losing your baby sister can't be compared to any other acquaintance, friend, or extended family member. I would prefer Mother Mary or Cain to die one hundred times over Jenna dying once.

What am I supposed to do now that she's gone? How

can I possibly survive without her? Even if the majority of our relationship lived in my head, how am I meant to go on?

The weight of reality hit me the second day back in Tampa. I awoke in the morning to a pain. My chest was tight, and my stomach felt like someone was squeezing it. As soon as my brain computed that it was a new day, I burst into tears.

I stayed in bed crying for weeks. During the brief intervals when it would stop, I tried to go to the kitchen to eat something or to the bathroom to take a shower.

Yet, halfway there, I would collapse on the floor and wail. My throat hurt from the sobbing, but I couldn't stop it from coming out. My eyes were swollen, but the tears flowed regardless.

After a month in the house, I tried going to the grocery store to grab a few essentials. I hadn't been eating because I was sick to my stomach every day. I wanted to find anything that might entice me to eat.

While in the tea aisle browsing some options, I burst into tears. I couldn't control my grief or the crying. When I cry, it's not cute. It isn't a droplet of water streaming down my cheek. Rather, it's a red face, a closed throat, gasps for air, vocal weeping, and a body collapsed on the floor.

I was embarrassed that there were people around who saw my ugly rupture of sadness. It was unmanageable yet no less humiliating. I abandoned my grocery basket and ran to the car. I waited until the tears subsided to drive home.

From that moment on, I was afraid to go out in public because I couldn't control my crying outbursts. I couldn't even dictate when they would start to come on so that I could at least begin running toward the exit. I was insuppressible and inconsolable. The only option was to isolate.

I tried taking drives around town to get out of the house, but it was the same thing. The tears weren't gentle streaks down my cheeks.

They were vision blurring and fire hydrant gushing, which made driving dangerous. Not that I cared much about living. I was glazed over and catatonic. It all seemed black.

I retreated to my bed to drown in grief. I stayed there watching movies and TV shows, scrolling on the internet, and only passing out when exhaustion overtook me. My bed, the house, it was the only place I felt safe.

Sleeping was difficult. Every time I closed my eyes, I would see Jenna in the viewing at the funeral home. Her stiff shell haunts me and makes sleep impossible. It felt as though I was still there. I could smell the room and feel the touch of her long, thick hair on my fingers.

Other times, when I closed my eyes, I would reenact certain events or conversations with her. I would fixate on how I could have been different. Perhaps if I had just gone to the gym with her more while she was in Nashville, she never would have died.

Maybe if I bought her that pair of shoes when she asked, she never would have died. Maybe if I had responded when she told me that she was cold, she never would have died.

Maybe if I had bought her stronger drugs while she was detoxing at my apartment, she never would have died. Maybe if I had never left home at sixteen, she never would have died.

The torment went on day and night. Time became an illusion, and I felt dead and trapped in hell. My phone was often in airplane mode, so no one could reach me.

I didn't want anyone to see me like this. I didn't want any more hollow words. These are the same words everyone says when someone dies, *"It's God's plan. It's for the best. She isn't suffering anymore. She's in a better place. She's free now."*

What the fuck about me, though? What about the pain that is suffocating me? What about the thoughts of her that haunt me? What about the fact that I don't want life without her? What about the fact that I am drowning in the ocean at night, and no one is around?

They mean well, but those words always come across as one-sided. Yes, they are in a better place, sure. But what about the place that I'm in?

Sleeping remained unattainable, and my eating was equally distorted. I would go days or weeks without eating, and then I would binge for days or weeks.

Sometimes, I couldn't bring myself to think about food at all. How could I? It was selfish to think about food during a time of mourning.

Then, when I would binge, it was in an effort to cope, to distract myself. An attempt to manage or numb the pain and anguish. Food and grocery delivery services became my friend. I never had to drive anywhere or risk being embarrassed in public. I could order anything at any time, and it would magically appear on my doorstep.

I'm no stranger to disordered eating. To cope with stress or highly emotional times, I will either stop eating or binge. Mother Mary would binge eat.

She would buy treats for herself and binge in front of Jenna and me. After she would binge, she would say, *"Why did you let me eat all that?"*

As if young children to an abusive parent were about to say something about her binge eating. She loved swiss rolls and oatmeal creme pies. She would buy a box of them at the grocery store.

We would sit in the car, in the parking lot, and watch as she ate the entire box. She would then express her disdain for what she had just done. I probably got my food and emotional coping from her. Food can also be a punishment.

I was once drugged and raped by someone that I knew. This led to a pregnancy and a very difficult decision. I had an abortion and felt devastated afterwards.

Not about my choice, but about being forced to make that choice. I never wanted an abortion because I never wanted to get pregnant. I certainly never wanted to be with the person who drugged me.

To cope with the stress, I stopped eating for about a year. I would eat an apple or a snickers bar and nothing else all day. I would also go to the gym for hours at a time.

The weight fell off very quickly, but I continued to refuse to eat. I was punishing myself. I did something awful, and part of my punishment was feeling the pain of extreme hunger.

I know it's far from healthy, but it's such a simple way to either feel pain or pleasure. I needed to feel a mix of both as it pertained to Jenna. It was the only thing I could control.

The months blurred on without any distinction between the present day and the day before. With my lack of sleep, I often couldn't tell what time of the day it was or which day of the week it was. Not that any of it mattered. I was fully engulfed with blackness, with grief, with pain.

The suffering began to breach my pain tolerance wall. My mind continued to refuse. Jenna was gone. Yet, when moments of reality drifted in, I would cry uncontrollably. I would pace, rock back and forth, or lay in the fetal position.

Finding a bit of courage, I wandered outside to get some fresh air. There it was again. A helium balloon in my yard. This has happened several times since Jenna's death.

The first one I found was a plain green helium balloon just off to the right of my front door. It appeared to be deciding if it wanted to sink or float. Wading in some kind of balloon limbo.

The next one I saw was a silver helium balloon stuck in a tree at the side of my house. I counted at least five or six various helium balloons either stuck in my yard or crossing my path. I've never seen any helium balloons in my yard before.

I'm not sure what happens after you die or how much you can interact with Earth. Or if it was even anything at all, but I took it as a sign from Jenna. I felt a little bit of comfort that she was here and she was okay.

One of the biggest things I struggled with was the last night that Jenna was alive. She caused a massive fight at Cain's house and attempted to attack a member of his second family. Cain decided to put her in a motel.

That night, from the motel, she had called Cain. She was scheduled to enter a rehabilitation center the following morning. They had discussed what time Cain would arrive at the motel to bring her to the treatment center.

Later on, Jenna called Mother Mary. She stated that Jenna was high, and the conversation didn't go that well. It was almost like Jenna knew in her gut to call Mother Mary one last time. She called Cain. She called Mother Mary. Yet, she never called me.

Why would she? We hadn't spoken in over a year. I wanted one last call, though. I wanted one last memory of her voice. High or not. She never said goodbye to me. She just left me. She left me alone.

Replaying her last night, and the phone call I wished I received, frequently echoed in my mind. Desperately wishing I could time travel and alter the events of her life. Even though it seems irrational to fantasize about traveling back in time, it consumed me.

After about nine months of being in my bed, I decided to start pet-sitting again. I needed to generate some income, and I also wanted to force myself out of the house. Since the job didn't require me to interact with people, I felt safe if a crying outburst occurred.

As I tried to force myself to reintegrate into society Jenna had been sending me messages. Well, maybe it was her, maybe it was God or the Universe, or maybe it was just me comforting myself. Each time there was a helium balloon in my yard or in my path, I would acknowledge it as a sign from her.

I often saw heart shapes, too. A heart-shaped rock under my foot, a droplet of water on the sink drain in the exact shape of a heart. A ripped piece of paper that was a jagged heart. I saw hearts in many places.

Since Cain's portion of Jenna's remains were placed in a specialty urn with monarch butterflies on it, I also saw monarch butterflies as a sign from her. I only ever noticed butterflies after Jenna died.

One even landed on my shoulder for a moment before it fluttered away into the distance. Sometimes I would see two of them in an acrobatic dance mid-air. Each time, I would stop and acknowledge that it could be or was from Jenna.

Even with subtle signs of Jenna's presence, the pain continued. My heart ached, and I felt deflated. Almost sunken into a crack where no one would ever notice my absence. I thought the turmoil would have eased by now, but I hadn't.

My obsessive thoughts of regret and replaying every aspect of my life pressed on. I was beginning to wonder if the pain was my new normal. I suppose it was always going to hurt, every moment of every day.

A friend had given me a bottle of muscle relaxers. My ultimate lover from my days of drug experimentation. There were a few times that I pulled the bottle down from the top shelf in the medicine cabinet.

At first, I only held the bottle in my hand. Tipping it upside down and then twisting it around in my hand. I watched as the pills bounced through the haze of the orange plastic bottle.

I progressed to opening the bottle and shaking it around as the pills danced in unison. Then, I would slowly shuffle one or two pills into my hand and feel the smooth capsules in my palm. What would happen if I took one? What would happen if I took two?

I hadn't taken any medications or substances for over six years. Not even a Tylenol on the worst day of my menstrual cycle. However, I really wanted to escape the grief of Jenna.

My entire body felt it, both externally and internally. I talked myself out of it but found the bottle in my hands once again not long after that.

I poured the entire contents out into my hand and stared at them. These pretty, glossy capsules offer so much gratification and ease. They feel like a warm hug, and I could really use one of those right now.

If I took all these pills, how long would it take to die? Would it be slow? Would it be peaceful? How long would it take for someone to find me?

My landlord was the most relaxed man I had ever met. One time, I couldn't remember whether I paid rent. It was already the end of the month, but I couldn't find any record as to whether I had.

I called him and left a voicemail. He never even called me back. I still don't know if I skipped a month.

I wouldn't be able to count on him to find me in a reasonable timeframe. It would easily be several months before he would come by. Even then, he might not investigate further.

You sometimes hear about people who die and aren't found until years later. All their bills were on autopay, and they didn't have any family or friends.

Imagine you die and aren't found until years later. Would that even matter to you, though? I couldn't decide whether or not that would matter to me, so I put the pills back in the bottle.

The next day, I threw them out as I put my trash on the curb for pickup. It was too tempting to keep in the house. If I hadn't been completely sober for the past six years, I would have taken them to at least dull the pain.

Ten months after Jenna died, I was at a client's condo. He lived on the eighteenth floor of a high-rise building downtown. It was a small dog that was older and wore diapers. He didn't need much care apart from some medicine, fresh food, water and a quick walk or two.

It was the evening, sometime after 9 PM, and I was washing my hands in the kitchen sink. The condo was open concept, and as I washed my hands, I looked over at the door to the balcony.

The next thing I knew, I was outside and swinging my legs over the balcony railing. I had no recollection of walking to the door, opening it or moving toward the railing. I stood on the ledge of the balcony, looking down at how tiny life was below me.

All this pain and suffering. I can't seem to make it go away. It feels like it's getting worse. I want to cry until time falls and existence ends. I want to wail every day so that the world hears my pain. I can't bear this agony anymore. It's too much.

Jenna was my everything, and now I have nothing. I am all alone in this world. No one understands me. I love no one on this Earth. What is the point of living? If I die, at least the pain will end. If I die, there is a sliver of possibility that I can see Jenna again, even if it's just for a moment.

I kept looking down, wondering how long it would take to make contact with the life below me. My heart was racing, but I was done feeling this pain and turmoil. My entire life has been dominated by pain and suffering, with only small glimpses of joy.

I'm tired of it all. I'm tired of having to be strong all the time. Why am I always asked to be strong? If there is a God, he is cruel and unkind. He tortures me and brings me to my knees in pain.

I was trying to build up the courage to let go of my grip on the balcony railing. All I needed to do was loosen my grip, and the suffering would be over. It would all end. I would be free. You battle with yourself when on the edge of your own existence.

Part of you wants to end it all. Yet, another part of you wants to live. The internal battle raged on as the tears fell from my cheeks and onto the life below me.

I continued trying to gather the courage to let go of the railing. The wind brushed against my cheeks, reminding me that I was teetering but still alive.

I was breathing rapidly and could feel my heartbeat in my throat. I wanted to die so that the pain would end. I was desperate for it to end. All of a sudden, a small voice popped into my head. It was that tiny voice. It sounded like my own but felt like it came from an external source.

The voice gently said in a neutral tone, *"If you do it, everyone will remember you as weak."*

I paused, wondering where that came from before angrily yelling, *"But I'm not weak. I'm always strong. I'm always forced to be the strong one. I'm tired of it. I can't do it anymore. It hurts too much."*

My mind raced between wanting to die and wanting to live. I just wanted the suffering to end, no matter how. I couldn't bear it anymore. Tears continued to stream down my face as I attempted to rouse enough courage to let go of the railing.

The same gentle and neutral tone spoke again, *"If you do it, everyone will remember you as weak."*

I am many things. You could say I am mean, selfish, impatient, greedy, lustful, angry, naïve, and much more. There would be many people who would agree with those words and then some.

However, the one thing you could never say about me. The one thing that no one would ever believe about me, is that I am weak. How could I be remembered for the one thing that I am not? I can't be remembered like that. I won't allow it.

My grip on the balcony railing tightened as I swung my legs back over. I rushed inside the condo, quickly locked the door and moved a table in front of it. My heart was still racing at what had just transpired. I couldn't decipher if I was happy or sad that I was still alive.

I took care of the dog for several more days and never once even glanced at that balcony again. The world will not remember me as weak. I won't give them the satisfaction.

Several weeks after the balcony event, I read a news article about a man who killed himself. His older brother was in the military and died during service. On the one-year anniversary of his older brother's death, the family held a remembrance ceremony.

The younger brother shot himself in the head after the ceremony. I've never related to anyone more in my life. The pain is something you cannot describe to others.

Losing your sibling when they are young, and in a tragic event, takes your soul from you. First your heart breaks and aches. You agonize over the physical and emotional pain. Then a hand busts through your ribcage, grabs hold of your heart, twists it, removes it from your body and walks away with it.

You wake up one day and realize that you are empty. A shell not too far removed from your deceased loved one. Your soul is gone. You feel nothing, want nothing, and hate everyone.

The first year after Jenna died, I spent it in my bed crying. Hoping that, eventually, the tears would stop or dry up. They never did, though.

Who knew that we have an endless supply of tears? It was nothing but a fever dream of despair, regret, heartache, disbelief, shock, and depression.

It was the darkest I had ever gone mentally. Sure, I have been through dark times. I have battled inner demons. I was once at war with myself and used work, university, and substances to distract me from the misery of my inner world.

I know what it's like to go dark in your mind. I know

what it's like to hate the world. I know what it's like to hate yourself.

This, however, was not even in the same realm as my previous experiences with darkness and turmoil. This was beyond anything I ever knew to be possible. It was beyond what I was capable of withstanding.

Each day the sun would rise was another day that I wished would go away. It was another day that I was to suffer and another day that I would punish myself with rumination. I tried my best to broaden my scope of life. It's supposed to all be by design, isn't it?

Everything is supposed to have a purpose, doesn't it? There is a God, right? If there was a God, why wouldn't he reach down and ease my pain? Why would he allow my heart to shatter in my chest without any aide whatsoever? The questions continued with no end in sight.

I wafted through the year in suffering as it all came to a head one evening. I collapsed to the floor of my bedroom and wailed in grief. I asked Jenna why she never said goodbye to me, like she said goodbye to Cain and Mother Mary.

I asked her why she hadn't come to me to tell me that she was safe in the spirit world. I asked for her forgiveness for my failures as a sister. I asked her why she had to leave me so early in life.

I screamed and cried until I felt delirious. On the floor,

rocking myself back and forth as I begged, pleaded, and prayed. A few moments passed, and I felt something come over me. It was calming and stopped my crying immediately.

As I stayed sitting on the floor with my eyes closed, I could see a lightly gray-colored shadow appear from a fog of bright white.

They weren't clouds, but they looked similar. I heard a neutral voice say, *"I'm ok. I am fine. Please don't cry anymore. I'm not mad at you. It's ok. Please, don't be so hard on yourself."*

It wasn't Jenna's voice, but it was almost as though it was a message delivered by a representative. The shadow also didn't feel as though it was Jenna, but it felt friendly. I begged for it to stay and for it to give me answers as to why this happened.

Why didn't she just get sober? Why did she leave without saying goodbye? Why didn't she tell me about her addiction sooner? There was silence.

The figure left without offering me anything more. I remained on the floor in exhaustion as the calmness lingered for several more minutes before dissipating. I crawled into bed and instantly fell asleep. It was the best sleep I had gotten in a year.

CHAPTER FOURTEEN

∴

"Grief looks a lot like anger on the outside. Sometimes it seems simply like unmerited rage, but it's really the frustration the heart feels when it finds itself in trauma that it can't make any sense of."

John Pavlovitz

The depth of my depression began to soften. I was able to go outside more often and eventually returned to working full-time. However, my experience shifted from despair to something else. I was now angry.

I'm not sure exactly when things changed for me, but at some point, I became incredibly angry. The world didn't care about how broken I was. It never paused to give me a moment to catch my breath. It hurt that my profound pain wasn't shared by anyone.

Cars whizzed past on the street. Horns honked at

distracted drivers. People strolled around the neighborhood. Children laughed and played. Stores bustled with customers. Construction crews built new buildings. People joked and laughed, movies debuted, and credit card bills arrived in the mail.

Life didn't even glitch. Not for a fraction of a second. I was furious at the world for making me suffer alone, for making me feel small and unheard, for forcing me to hide my torment in shame.

Society doesn't like angry people, yet no one ever asks why they're angry in the first place. Especially in today's world, videos flood the internet of people consumed by their emotions, cracking, lashing out.

Yet, all anyone does is record them to share online, where the world laughs at their misery. To mock someone for feeling anything. For having a bad day, a bad week, or even a bad year.

We're shamed for holding in our pain, but no one wants to hear about it. What are we supposed to do with it, the rage that boils inside us with nowhere to go.

Responsibilities don't pause for anger: jobs, bills, shopping, relationships, car maintenance, life's endless demands march on. For those of us who are drowning, why are we the ones mocked and shunned? We're already hurt, broken, and disconnected.

From its onset, the anger inside me felt dangerously close to the surface. It needed to be expelled. The smallest annoyance became an excuse to release my pent-up aggression, traffic, long lines, a sideways glance, an accidental nudge in public, no parking spaces, people misusing traffic circles, anything. There wasn't a reason not to react with excessive force.

I had no healthy way to manage the anger within me. How do you get rid of it? How do you channel it constructively? No one discusses anger, especially anger in women. We're not *"meant"* to be angry, so it's treated as if it doesn't exist. If it doesn't exist, there's no outlet for it.

I, however, was an angry woman. I wanted to light a match, watch the world burn, and revel in the collapse. The intensity of my anger was uncontrollable.

A perceived slight from a grocery store cashier could set off a massive blow-up. One outburst led to another, and then another.

I was frenzied and detached from myself. I didn't know who I was anymore. I felt like nothing without Jenna. Life seemed insignificant in my separation from it. Nothing but pain and rage vibrated through me. It was me.

While out running errands one afternoon I decided to treat myself to a drink at a popular coffee chain. I rarely went there, but I thought it might lift my mood. I ordered a chai latte and waited. I was the only customer waiting, so I couldn't understand why it was taking so long.

After five minutes, I asked the barista about my order. She snapped that drinks were made in the order they were received, a snide smirk accompanying her words. That smirk ignited something in me.

Moments later, the next order was called, an order for someone who had arrived after me. That was it. I returned to the same barista, who curtly informed me my drink was already on the counter. They hadn't even called my name.

I couldn't control myself. I hated her. I hated that store. I hated that latte. I grabbed my chai, removed the lid, and splashed it all over the floor near the entrance.

I made it look like an accident, except for the dramatic way I tossed the empty cup on the floor as I walked out. It cost me $6.25, but it felt worth it. Fuck her. Fuck that place. Fuck that latte.

Once something set me off, I was rampant. It was as if another entity, the broken, wailing part of me, took over, demanding the world acknowledge my wrath. Once I calmed down, I felt a faint twinge of guilt.

I was slightly embarrassed by my behavior, but only because it was witnessed publicly. Privately, I wouldn't have hesitated to do it again. I guess I was sorry, but not that sorry.

The emotional state that I was in, couldn't comprehend how the world pressed on regardless of my grief. It was bitter that no one else appeared to be suffering like I was. Everything was normal and there was something wrong with me because I wasn't.

It reminded me of my childhood. How I was supposed to pretend like I wasn't hurting. How Jenna was rewarded for pretending and I was punished for revealing the truth. It was playing out over again except this time it was bigger. It was me against the world.

Pet sitting kept me busy and forced me to leave the house and take walks. It helped to reduce the obsessive thoughts about Jenna.

When I had easy clients, I would relax on their couches, watch Netflix, eat their snacks, and take naps. Having money roll back into my bank account was a good thing, and a bit of a relief.

I continued to keep my distance from friends and acquaintances. If I was forced to interact with anyone, I did my very best to put on a front like everything was fine.

Most people had no idea my baby sister had died. I kept it that way because I wanted to spare them from giving me those sad, pitying eyes.

The truth was, I was so volatile that I felt ashamed to be around anyone I knew for extended periods of time. It wasn't a matter of if my aggression would boil over, it was when. I didn't want to show that to anyone I cared about. I wasn't myself.

Then again, maybe my normal self had died alongside Jenna. Perhaps I was now only a remnant of what was or what could have been. That was still to be determined. If this state was temporary, it was best for anyone I knew to stay far away from me. They wouldn't understand.

Walking around in an extreme state of grief, with ferocious anger, feeling as though no one understands, that is an isolated place to live. It makes you hate the world even more.

It terrified me that I wasn't able to control my anger. I was afraid of morphing into Mother Mary. I didn't want my beautiful green eyes to turn black like hers.

In the past, no one had come to save me. I could already tell this experience would be no different especially since I kept everyone at a distance. Surviving out of spite might just be the only thing keeping me alive.

I decided to buy some cheap dinnerware at a second-hand store, the mismatched stock no one wanted. I could relate to those misfit pieces pushed to the back, left unseen. Perhaps collecting dust and ultimately at the end of their existence.

I picked the ones that looked the saddest. One single

saucer, a chipped plate, three teacups, a serving dish at the bottom of a stack. I even grabbed a Christmas themed coffee cup with an image of Santa Claus on it.

One night, when I was particularly upset, I loaded the dinnerware into my car and drove around until I found a deserted parking lot with a dumpster.

I got out of my car and placed the dishes on the ground. I stood staring at the dumpster taking slow, deep breaths. While I contemplated what I was about to do, I looked down at those sad, pathetic dishes.

Grabbing the chipped dinner plate, I held it to my chest, closed my eyes and felt the sadness. Allowing the pain, hopelessness, rage and sorrow to vibrate through every cell of my body. I waited until it radiated through my lungs, expelling outward with every breath.

My grip on the plate tightened and I allowed my emotions to transfer to it. Tears began to stream down my cheeks and my face wrinkled with distress. Holding the plate with both hands I raised it above my head, took one big inhale and hurled it toward the dumpster.

I waited until I heard it collide, shattering into thousands of pieces in a symphony of chaos. Something inside of me unleashed as I hastily reached for another misfit plate. The smashing continued one after the other without pause, or caution.

Each moment the plates made impact was a moment of release. Small pieces of my torment felt heard, seen, real. I wasn't imagining my suffering. It was no longer invisible. The world was forced to bear witness to it, shattered into thousands of pieces.

I began to grunt with each throw, which quickly turned into screams. Tears erupted from my eyes, blurring my vision, but I continued. Throwing, screaming, and smashing until every single piece of dinnerware was gone.

Wiping my eyes, I scanned the results of what I had done. Most of the dinnerware never made it to the dumpster. The parking lot looked lawless, mad, and confusing. It looked how I felt ever since Jenna died.

Making my way back to the car, I crumpled into the seat and wailed, screaming to the sky, *"Why did you leave me? You fucking left me. WHY??!! You never even said goodbye. You never loved me! Fuck you!"*

I screamed until my throat felt raw and broken from the rage that boiled within me. Emphasizing each word with every bit of energy that I could conjure. The outburst left me exhausted, deflated and defeated.

I hated Jenna for leaving me like that, so abruptly, so dysfunctional, so dramatically. She left me all alone, with no regard for what my life would be like without her. How was I supposed to live without her?

The desperation inside of me rose. Once my tears dried enough for me to see again, I started the car and drove home.

For about six months, I worked at a kebab shop while living in Australia. It was run by a Greek man named George, who had a very thick accent. He was older, joyous, and relaxed, never taking anything too seriously.

Every Saturday night, George brought in several boxes of dishes. The shop stayed open late into the night, and George let us smash the dishes in a corner of the dining room.

Employees and customers alike joined in. He'd turn on traditional Greek music, dance around, and start smashing dishes before handing a few to others to join the fun.

Not only was it exciting smashing those dishes but it was also cathartic. Any tension between employees would dissipate as we smashed dishes next to one another. Liability concerns? Who knows. It didn't matter to George. He acted as though he was the law.

I'll always remember George and those dishes. The glee and brightness he brought to the shop. Perhaps that's why my first thought was to smash dinnerware. It brought temporary relief.

I also tried throwing eggs to release my fury. I'd buy eggs on clearance, find a secluded place in the woods or along a trail and smash them one at a time.

Crying, screaming, grunting, until the carton was empty. It felt good but only for a short period of time. Nevertheless, the destruction was satisfying.

My thoughts were always on Jenna though. I couldn't stop ruminating on how I could have changed the outcome of her life. How messed up our circumstances were.

How disappointing life had been for her. All the ways I could have possibly banished the demons that resided within her.

What if our doctor had reported Mother Mary? Would Jenna still be here? What would our lives have looked like?

I desperately wanted to know. I imagined every scenario possible, and they all ended with Jenna still alive.

All I could think about was my sweet, innocent Jenna and how life had failed her. How Cain had failed her. How Mother Mary had failed her. How she failed herself.

I couldn't help but wonder how Jenna would have turned out if we'd come from a loving home. If we'd been *"normal."* Jenna had an alluring personality. She was fun and social, with a natural ability to manipulate people.

If she'd come from love, she might have been too

dangerous for this world, charming it into submission and leaving it wondering what had just happened. It would've been breathtaking to see her shine her light on the world, though.

People say that living in the past takes you nowhere. That fantasizing about false possibilities is a waste of energy. Yet it's all I seem capable of. My life revolves around Jenna and what could have been. My heart aches for those endless possibilities.

I also think about advice I never took while Jenna was actively addicted. A friend from India suggested chaining her up in the house for a few months so she could detox. I thought about that idea. I thought about our brief conversation regarding it.

"Just lock her in the house. Chain her if you need to," he advised.

"Chain her? That's kidnapping. It's illegal. What if the police find out?" I replied in utter shock at the suggestion.

"The police? What's it their business? It's your sister, your family. She could die," he replied.

It was a crazy suggestion. It almost felt illegal just to think about let alone talk about. As shocked as I was, I did consider it for about a day.   Her addiction left me distraught, and I took everything under advisement. I remember thinking about how I might have done it.

I would need to find a basement or a house that was secluded. I would have to chain her because she would definitely try to escape. If I chained her, I would need to monitor her either personally or with a video camera.

I wondered if Mother Mary's house would be secluded enough? Mother Mary wouldn't be strong enough to allow for such a thing. It would have to be in another location. I would have to manage it alone.

As outrageous as that idea was, I often wonder why I didn't at least try it, maybe it could've worked. My friend knew families in India who did similar things, and it turned out successful for them.

What if we could have been successful too? Now, I'll never know. I regret not trying. At least then I could've said I'd done everything possible, everything suggested.

I finally decided to purchase customized jewelry with Jenna's fingerprint on it. I chose her middle fingerprint. I bought a pendant with her print and a signet pinky ring as well.

I thought buying jewelry in her memory might help me feel better. It didn't change how I felt, but I still wore them every day.

Jenna and I used to flip each other off in a joking manner. We would pop around corners, flipping up our middle fingers, jeering, *"Fuck you, motherfucker."*

We played with the way we flipped each other off and how we called each other motherfucker. It was a silly game, and I have fond memories of us doing it. On the back of the pendant, I had them engrave: middle fingers to the sky.

It was in honor of our game, but it was also partially genuine, fuck you in a playful way, and fuck you for leaving, in a serious way.

As the anger inside me continued to simmer, I started to dislike who I had become, who I was forced to embody. I used to be relaxed, happy, and content. I meditated, practiced yoga, and smiled at strangers. Now, I was the opposite. I felt like a stranger to myself and feared what it meant for my future.

Who could love an angry woman? Who would want to be near someone like that? I didn't want to be near myself. My isolation grew, and my disdain for the world expanded.

I found myself at a gas station one afternoon. I had been feeling especially upset that week, mostly sad, crying a lot. The tears came in waves.

Some days or weeks, I cried nonstop; other times, not as much. I couldn't control it. I just had to ride it out, even when I felt defeated.

That day, I was feeling particularly low, so I decided to buy a couple of lottery tickets, in an attempt to cheer myself up. When I entered the store, the employee was immediately rude.

At the counter, I greeted her while eyeing the scratch-off display to decide what I wanted. She responded with a dismissive sound. I was already feeling sensitive, but I tried to focus.

I had difficulty communicating exactly what I wanted. I knew I wanted a Powerball ticket, but the words wouldn't come to me. It was as though my mind had gone blank. I stood there, struggling to retrieve a thought.

Then the employee snapped, her tone sharp, *"I need to see your ID."*

"ID? For what?" I asked, startled.

"For cigarettes. I see you lookin','" she grunted.

I was confused. I don't smoke. Why would she think I wanted cigarettes? Had I asked for them without realizing it? No, I was sure I hadn't. Finally, I managed to say, *"You don't see me lookin' at anything,"* pointing to the sunglasses I was wearing.

"What do you want, then?" she demanded as she leaned her body closer to me.

I felt utterly defeated. Why couldn't I communicate that I wanted a Powerball ticket. Why had my mind gone blank? My heart ached with grief. My chest burned with frustration. My throat closed with fear.

I was like a small child struggling to babble words that just wouldn't come. Desperate to speak, yet unable to formulate a sentence. To tell her I wanted a Powerball ticket. Or to even tell her to fuck off with her damn attitude.

The anger boiled up inside me. I knew this feeling. I just didn't know what was about to happen. I could feel my skin peel back. I lost control.

Before I could blink, I grabbed a tall snack display beside me and flung it at her. Boxes of candy by my thighs? I hurled those too. I shoved the small counter displays in her direction and stormed out. I said nothing. I couldn't find any words.

She screamed for her manager and for someone to call the cops. I walked to my car, started it, and drove off. Nothing ever came of that event, but I wanted to hurt her. I wanted to jump behind the counter and punch her, to rip her cheap wig off and bash her until I saw blood.

That desire, for blood from a stranger, terrified me. The rage inside me was reaching a point where I might not be able to control it next time. What happens if I can't control it next time? Am I Mother Mary?

I needed help, outside help. I had never experienced grief or rage this all-encompassing. Nothing had ever come close. Since I didn't have health insurance, I scoured Groupon for any deals and found a counselor offering two sessions for $50. I purchased it and made my first appointment for the following week.

I've always prided myself on being strong, independent, and tenacious. I don't see much value in others; too many people have let me down, abandoned me, rejected me, or cast me aside. Admitting I couldn't do it alone was agonizing.

Truthfully, I'd spent years working with therapists and psychologists to heal from my childhood. They had helped in some ways, but most were pill pushers, insistent on keeping me medicated. My last experience with professional mental health services had been disappointing, but right now, I needed help.

When the appointment came, we met over a video conference. It was my first time meeting a mental health professional virtually. It felt less personal but far more convenient. She asked what brought me to her, and I explained everything in a quick yet sufficient manner.

The sessions were only an hour, so I didn't want to waste half the time recounting my story. I needed solutions, practical advice. I poured my heart out for ten solid minutes, tears streaming down my face as I pushed through. Once I finished, she paused and said, *"I can't help you."*

My heart sank. My skin tingled. I knew it. No one can

help me. I'm beyond help. I'm on my own. What do you do when no one can help you, and you also can't help yourself?

Am I meant to suffer alone? Am I destined to wait until I draw blood from a stranger in a fit of rage? Her words echoed in my mind as despair overtook me.

After a long pause, she added, *"I can't help you because I'm going through something similar. My younger sister died from an overdose two years ago, and I'm still processing it. Some days are better than others. It's a conflict of interest."*

She proceeded to tell me all about her sister, how she had been sober for several months before relapsing, how she'd gotten a sleeve tattoo to commemorate her sister, even showing it to me on camera.

She talked for twenty minutes straight. I tried to be present for her; she clearly needed someone to confide in. I stayed strong for her, letting her say what she needed to.

A part of me hoped she might drop some pearls of wisdom as she spoke, but she didn't. When she finally finished, she informed me that she'd refund my money and apologized for not being able to help. We parted ways, and I closed my laptop, sitting in stunned silence trying to compute what just happened.

What the actual fuck was that? I'm on the verge of serious vengeance, and this professional turned our session into a monologue about herself. Why is it always me who's asked to be strong? Always. What about me? When is it my turn to receive? To be supported?

It took so much strength to reach out, and it was a catastrophic failure. No one can help me. I am hopeless. I am alone. Once again, it's just me and my darkness. Alone, drowning in an ocean at night.

It took days to recover from that interaction. It was hard to conceive just how alone I was, just how broken I had become. I stayed in bed more. Attempting to sleep away the days. I was safe in my bed.

I was mentally checked out and didn't care if I died. In fact, I wanted to die. I just knew I couldn't do it myself. Maybe being reckless would let me die naturally. I allowed myself to think about that for a while. How could I set myself up to die?

After a few days of contemplation, I decided to learn how to ride a motorcycle. They're dangerous, especially in Tampa, where no one looks when they merge, and accidents happen daily. It felt like a way to die adventurously.

I signed up for a three-day motorcycle class. The first day was bookwork and instructions. The second was practical, and we rode motorcycles. The last day was split between a written exam and a practical test. I passed both and bought a motorcycle within weeks of getting my license endorsed.

I found a 1989 Honda Hawk 650cc from a private seller in St. Petersburg who happened to work at a motorcycle shop. I took an Uber there and inspected the bike. I was tremendously nervous to test drive it.

Being overcome by fear, I asked an older guy, that was browsing the store, if he could test drive the bike. He obliged and assured me it was a good bike, so I bought it.

My first time driving a motorcycle on the street was a nerve-wracking 45-minute ride on a main highway. In the class, we were in a parking lot now I was on the road.

I made it back with only a few clutch mistakes. I felt alive. For the first time since Jenna died, I was living.

The only time I felt relief from my anger was when I smashed dishes, glasses, or eggs. The only time I felt truly alive was when I rode my motorcycle. It wasn't the healthiest way to cope, but it was all I had.

Despite the darkness that still clouded my days and the regret that haunted my nights, time passed. One day after another.

Until I woke up one morning and realized the pain of losing Jenna had subsided. It wasn't as sharp anymore. Days had passed without thinking about her or her death.

You might think that brought me hope, but instead, I felt guilty. A portion of me did want to feel better, for the aggression to go away, for the heartache to dull. Yet, the realization that the memory of Jenna was beginning to fade made me feel like a horrible person.

Shouldn't I mourn her for the rest of my life? Shouldn't I wear black and weep daily? Am I a bad sister for letting her become a distant memory?   I wanted to cry every day until my own death. I wanted the world to feel my loss. I wanted Jenna to dominate every moment of my life.

The guilt was intense, making me feel like a bad person. A failure of a sister, yet again. Some nights, I would force Jenna into my mind, intentionally becoming sad and crying. I would force the image of her during the funeral viewing into my head at night, so that I wouldn't sleep.

I wanted myself to suffer. I wanted the suffering to remain because it meant that I loved her and that her essence would never die.

How else are you supposed to commemorate the greatest love of your life? How else are you supposed to honor the only person in the entire world whom you would die for?

Grief is odd. You want the pain to go away, but when it does, you want it to come back. At least come back and remain at some low-grade level of discomfort.

Anytime I felt myself forgetting about Jenna or moving on with my life, I would pull myself back. I would force the darkness to return.

After I had that abortion in my early twenties, I

stopped eating as a punishment. Here I am doing it again, punishing myself for Jenna's death by not allowing myself to heal.

I stayed in that state of mind for many months. The moment I noticed that I felt good or hadn't thought about her in several days, I would bring the darkness back to the forefront.

Perhaps I deserved it, though. Perhaps, in many ways, I did fail Jenna. I was a bad sister. I didn't save her like I should have. I couldn't find a way to reach her. I deserved to suffer for an undisclosed amount of time.

Everyone always talks about the five stages of grief. They act as if you progress straight through them in order, and at the end you will be magically healed.

"Just work through the stages," they always say. *"It's a process."*

If that were true, then my process was in disarray. I was stuck in anger, and no one seemed to have anything productive to say or do about it.

Some of the stages were mixing, bargaining spilling over into anger, and depression contaminating everything. It was mucky as I tried my best to dredge through in spite.

Perhaps I was just unreachable. I was too enthralled with the pain, making it impossible for any outside voice to reach me.

The last stage of grief is acceptance. I never wanted to reach that stage, anyway. I never wanted any of this to be true. I wanted to suffer so greatly that I simply melted away.

As time continued to pass, life slowly returned to normal, I couldn't stop it. I began allowing myself to spend time in public or to go to the gym. Jenna's memory continued to fade, too. I hated that she was fading.

No one will remember her in a few years. She'll be nothing more than a figment of our imaginations, a memory that seems like it stemmed from a past life, a distant time that you no longer associate with. My sweet, innocent baby Jenna was disappearing.

Even when I tried to force her memory back, she wasn't as clear in my mind. When I tried extra hard, she would only pop in and then quickly fade away.

Perhaps this was part of acceptance. I was being forced into the final stage of grief, whether I liked it or not.

Death is challenging to overcome, but fading memories are also difficult to accept. I never wanted her to fade. I never wanted to go days, weeks, or months without thinking about her. I was wedged between the desire for less suffering and maintaining the strong memory of my sister.

Even though thinking about her brought me intense heartache. It was a reminder of a failure. Of a lost love. Of my own loneliness in the world now that I had no one who understands me. Now that there is no one on this Earth that I love.

As Jenna faded, another sentiment seemed to creep in. If Jenna is no longer here and I no longer care if I die, then what really matters? What actually matters?

I had stopped caring about life and whether it had any meaning. I always wanted to do good so that I could be an example for Jenna, so that she could look at me as a role model of what was possible.

Everything I did was for her to see. For her to have a person in her life who came from the same place and overcame.

Now that Jenna is no longer here, who am I setting an example for? Why would I achieve anything? Why would I remain sober? Why would I chase dreams and take chances? Who is it for now? There is no one here. No one to showcase to.

Nothing has any meaning now. I care much less about others, about looking a certain way or acting a certain way. I moved from wanting the world to being impartial to it. It's a meaningless place, and no one matters.

People are superficial and unimportant. I no longer wanted to hurt anyone, but I certainly wasn't interested in interacting with them.

I rode the motorcycle a little more recklessly. I cut

people off in traffic. I stopped greeting people. I gave people an attitude when they would try to strike up conversations with me. I would give a death stare to strangers who smiled at me.

I hardly allowed pedestrians to cross the street as I drove around. I sped in my car and did burnouts around corners. I blasted profane music near busy playgrounds. I bought a microphone for the car and trolled people with the windows down and the volume on full blast.

Since I no longer cared about being a good citizen, I no longer wanted to participate in the general rules of society. I wanted to be separate from it. Society never honored my sweet Jenna; therefore, I no longer wanted to honor society.

I no longer had a reason for playing by the rules. If Jenna could no longer see me, then what was the use? To be honest, I felt like a troubled teenager again. I was reckless, vocal, disruptive, and it was freeing.

I had a lot of angst as a teenager, and it was easy to reconnect with that version of myself, the misfit who never conformed, so she excavated her own ditch to play in.

Now I had an opportunity to play in that very same ditch again. Though, a little less reckless. A little less vocal. A little less disruptive.

Let's be honest, I do have bills to pay and I'm not interested in going to jail. The circumference and depth of the ditch are slightly smaller these days. Let it be known, though, that the ditch still does, very much, exist.

CHAPTER FIFTEEN

∴

"One foot in front of the other. Repeat as often as necessary to finish."
Haruki Murakami

J enna's absence now meant that I was free to travel. Though my heart was heavy, my wandering spirit was beginning to return. Part of me wanted to be rash, wanted to flee to a nondescript place. Hide away from the past and, if I was lucky, from myself.

That would be the easy way out though. Those decisions always come back to haunt you, and I didn't want anything left lingering in the air. Instead of fleeing I decided to take a trip out west to Utah to go hiking. Being in nature makes me feel connected to something bigger than myself.

The grief of Jenna left me isolated and feeling alone. However, I wanted to feel small in comparison to the Universe. I wanted my agony to be eclipsed by something bigger. For it to feel as though it either has a purpose or isn't the totality of my existence.

A secondary reason for the trip was to begin scattering her ashes. I'm not exactly sure where she would have wanted them, but I'm the keeper, so it's my decision now.

I want to scatter her at all the beautiful places around the world that I visit. Places that we could have explored together if things were different.

When we were younger, we talked about death. We had a very specific conversation about what we would want once we died. I remember having that conversation, but I could never remember what she said her preference was.

Did she want to be buried or cremated? That conversation has always been cloudy to me. I have some regrets about that.

Maybe she never even wanted to be cremated in the first place. Here I am, scattering pieces of her around the world. Another part of me wonders if a soul even cares, though. After your time has ended, would you really be worried about your wishes?

I couldn't shake the fact that Jenna never left her hometown. She never went on epic adventures or saw the wonders of the world. Keeping her ashes stuck in a plastic container felt like a continuation of this travesty.

Her addiction kept her chained to a small area, in her

death, she was freed. I wanted to ensure that this freedom extended to what was left of her physical form.

I packed a small backpack and brought along a sandwich bag with some of Jenna's remains. It felt borderline disrespectful to kept her in such a way. She might be looking down on me, laughing at either the bag or my conflicted thoughts.

Jenna and I made it to Utah without any problems. I got into the rental car and set off to explore the national parks. It was the beginning of our very first adventure together.

As a New Hampshire native, I love the mountains, hiking, and dense nature. Florida lacks all of that. Everything is flat and resembles a jungle. Utah, on the other hand, is a hiker's paradise. Outdoor activities are a part of everyone's normal routine, it's a big aspect of the lifestyle.

I made my way from Las Vegas to Zion National Park, then to Bryce Canyon National Park. This was by far the best park. The rock formations felt out of this world.

It felt like a sci-fi movie. The main trail was free to access and was an eight-mile-long loop. The beginning half was the best, and then it tapered off.

The long hike allowed me to disappear and become fully absorbed by the sites. I was insignificant next to the massive rock formations that reached toward the sky.

They had survived thousands of years and were still

standing tall. Their shapes had changed, but they remained.

The internal conflict of not feeling like I don't have a place in the world, mixed with the desire to be part of it, was something I continued to battle. This trip was an opportunity for me to realign. To find this new version of me.

As the trip continued, I explored Capitol Reef National Park, followed by Canyonlands National Park and Arches National Park. From there, I went to the Four Corners Monument and into New Mexico before looping back.

Each park had something different to offer. Whether it was tall rock formations, winding dirt roads through canyons, or sprawling archways. They were all magnificent and represented fundamental aspects of life.

The tall rock formations reminded me to endure and proceed even if I am changed by events or circumstances. The winding roads through canyons showed me that straight roads are boring and offer no opportunity for excitement or interesting stories.

The archways conveyed the significance of connection and bridging gaps. Even the Four Corners Monument spoke to the value of meeting others exactly where they are.

This was the first time I had ever visited Utah and now I understood what drew me here. I was able to find not only connection through nature but also meaning. It was calming and relaxing but also invigorating.

I had to move on from my grief because that's what nature does. It moves. It will move whether you like it or not. Whether you choose to participate or not.

The high elevation and intense trail inclines left me feeling exhausted which meant that I was alive. I endured and, like the rock formations, I was still standing.

I wondered if Jenna was watching as I explored the terrain with her ashes in my backpack. As I pondered life, my existence, and the meaning of it all.

In preparation for the trip, I wrote a list of all the places I wanted to visit. One of those places was called The Wave. While visiting the Carlsbad Caverns National Park in New Mexico, I got to talking with one of the rangers. I told him my plan to see The Wave.

He informed me that you need a permit, and that it's only given through a lottery-style drawing. He said that he had been living in the area for over a decade and tried for a permit every year but had never gotten it.

The chances were slim, according to him, but that didn't deter me. I must have missed the part about needing a permit and that it was a lottery-style drawing, too. I searched online and found where the lottery was being held, then made my way back into Utah.

The lottery took place at a school auditorium, and it was jam-packed when I arrived. A huge crowd of people filled the entryway as everyone chaotically grabbed an entry form. I filled out the application, submitted it, and took a seat in the stands to wait for the winners to be called.

I really wanted to see The Wave, but there were a lot of people here trying to get a permit. They only pulled eight numbers, so the odds were not in my favor. I sat waiting, feeling detached.

I assumed I wouldn't get it, but I wanted to see who did. As the drawing began, the woman spun a bingo wheel and pulled out the first winner: number ninety-six.

I looked down at the wrinkled paper stub between my fingers, creased from being folded and unfolded several times. My eyes shifted into focus to read what was printed in bold black ink.

I was number ninety-six. I jumped up from my seat, waving my hands in the air, yelling, *"Me! Me! That's me!"*

The crowd broke out in cheers as everyone clapped with eagerness. I couldn't believe it. Not only did I win, but I was the first one to be picked. I felt Jenna with me as I glanced around the auditorium at hundreds of smiling faces.

I'm pretty sure she orchestrated this because luck seemed inferior in this situation. I took it as a sign that she wanted some of her ashes scattered at The Wave.

Once the drawing was over, the participants were quickly shuffled toward the exit while the winners stayed for a safety briefing. It was a scary brief, too. They mentioned dying a few too many times for comfort.

I was having second thoughts because I hadn't seen anything online about dying due to dehydration or getting lost. We had to sign a waiver, and then they gave us our permits.

Hiking to The Wave wasn't too difficult, but it was a long hike, and there was no cell phone reception. I had downloaded the offline map and tried to use that as a guide to lead the way. I got lost a few times as I attempted to navigate around cliffs and when the trail seemed to taper in and out of distinction.

I might have taken the long way but eventually found The Wave. It felt like a mirage as I made my way up the sandy incline toward it. The final obstacle to overcome.

All I could see was a massive orange-brown chunk of rock that looked out of place. A desolate formation all alone in the middle of nowhere. I connected with the rock and its singularity.

Initially I was disappointed. The rock was dull, bland and unimpressive. I wondered what all the fuss was about. Why you needed a permit and why hundreds of people want to come here every day. It took several hours to hike here, and I was starting to feel like it was for nothing.

A found a small crack in the rock that looked like a

Amanda Bourque

hallway leading me into the heart of the formation.

I entered, walking inside the dull, dusty mound. The more I progressed the more it began to reveal itself to me. What looked ugly on the outside was only for those who dared not to go in.

The more I drew closer to the center the more beautiful the rock became. The sandstone transmuted into a pattern of color that varied with each thin layer.

It was smooth and curved like an ocean wave. There were large openings and smaller, more intimate ones. The patterns, colors, and curves varied at each section.

When I arrived, there was only one other person there, which made it an even better experience. It was quiet and felt private. He even offered to take my photo as I climbed up one of the wave crests for a better view.

Continuing to explore, I slowly made my way through the formation, taking photos, and admiring the mesmerizing grandeur of nature. I felt small, insignificant. It was exactly what I wanted. I wasn't everything, but rather I was a small part of something.

As the name suggests, it's called The Wave because the sandstone looks like ocean waves that would make any surfer euphoric. It was created by changing wind patterns, which shifted sand dunes that were slowly accumulated layer by layer over millions of years. This gives the formations a pattern of texture and color variance.

It was more stunning than the photos online. The intense orange, red, and brown hues along each wavy layer. It curved, turned, and rotated in a magical formation that left me astonished.

To me, it represented life, the twists and turns, the layers, the various colors and hues, the unexpected formations. The fact that it's reminiscent of the ocean reminded me to relax and enjoy the journey. Life is a ride, and the only way I'll survive it is by being loose and adaptable.

While wandering around, I found a small corner that felt safe enough to leave a part of Jenna. My hands trembled as I reached in my backpack to retrieve the sandwich bag. I pulled apart the closure, reached my fingers inside and pinched, making sure not to take too much.

I have to ration her ashes. Jenna will be with me for the rest of my life. We have a lot of places to visit.

My heart was racing as I looked at the grey remnants between my fingers. That was her. Jenna was in my hands, literally. I closed my eyes and took a deep breath, holding it for a few moments before slowly exhaling. My chest felt tight as I prepared myself for what I had come to do.

Jenna brought me to The Wave for a reason, and I needed to be strong for her. I took out my phone and made a video as I said a few words in her honor.

My pinched fingers were in the frame as I slowly opened them and watched as she drifted away. The wind took hold of her, and she danced for a moment before settling. This was a final goodbye to a small piece of Jenna.

As the trip continued, I sprinkled some of Jenna's ashes into the Rio Grande and the Grand Canyon as well. Each time felt equally as difficult, but she deserves to see the world. I always wanted to travel with her, but she always turned me down.

Now, she has no choice. She's being held captive in my backpack, and she will travel with me. She will forever live on in all the places we visit together.

As life continued, I felt myself beginning to step away from my re-lived teenage angst. Utah helped me realize that even though Jenna was no longer physically here, I know she is with me in other forms, energetically or metaphysically, however one might call it. I feel her and I hope that she can still see me.

I realized that I can't honor her by dismantling my life or sabotaging myself with pain and grief. I can still make her proud, and I can still carve a path, regardless of whether or not I can see her.

I tried my best to adopt this mentality, rearranging how I moved through the world and allowing myself the opportunity to advance into the future. I had really lost myself when Jenna died. Everything I loved about me and my life evaporated.

I was lost for a long time. Even though I am not back to how I was before, I could feel myself elevating. I allowed myself to disinfect and bandage the wounds so that I could finally heal and move on.

Depression seemed to come and go in much smaller and more manageable bouts. Sometimes it lasted several weeks, other times a month or two. I couldn't always identify the source, but I knew it was because I was still finding my way.

I felt myself still sloshing around seeking something, trying to find a missing item or two. What made it even more difficult was that I didn't know what I was seeking. I allowed myself to feel the sadness, to be directionless, to wade in the ocean until I figured it out.

I allowed myself the opportunity to be hopeless or frustrated or angry without attaching anything else to it. I knew I was going to get through it and that this was the last echo of bereavement.

Even though I felt the end was near, there was one particular bout of depression that scared me. It lingered for well over two months.

I felt myself being sucked back into the days directly following Jenna's death, the days of not leaving my bed and crying until my eyes were swollen. I had no desire to go outside, take a shower, wash the dishes, or do anything else for that matter.

I grew afraid that I might try to kill myself again. Maybe this time I would succeed. I'd drawn myself out of depression several times before. Usually by giving myself some time to be absorbed by the sadness. Just allowing whatever needed to be experienced to come to the surface. After some time, I always tried to reintroduce myself to the world.

I cleaned the house, did yard work, exercised, danced, went for a walk, called a friend, or signed up for a course or class. If those things didn't work, I'd try something scary, like swimming in the ocean (which is scary because I can't swim), driving recklessly, racing cars, skydiving, or other intense activities. This gets my heart racing to resurrect my desire for survival.

However, nothing seemed to work this time. None of my usual tactics were enticing enough. I was afraid, and I didn't want to reach out for help either.

Partly because I'm stubborn and don't need anyone's help, and partly because the last time I reached out for help, it fell on deaf ears.

It's embarrassing and reinforcing to ask for help and not get it. I felt dumb for thinking someone could help me, which also deepened my fear that no one could. Isolation became the loudest voice in my head.

I tried to get myself to clean the house for just ten minutes or even take a walk around the house, but the darkness prevailed. My body felt dense and heavy, as though it were weighted down and I couldn't move. I lost all caring for anything at all, including myself. Nothing mattered, and life had no point.

I tried being patient with myself, allowing the darkness to move through me in its own time. Yet, I never knew exactly when it would pass or when was enough. I straddled being compassionate with myself and being enveloped with darkness.

For this particular episode, I tried at least three times to pull myself out of it, to no avail. I began wondering how much deeper I would sink into despair. Would I evaporate into time?

One night, while pondering this, I fell to my knees and cried out, *"What more do you want from me? How much more do I have to endure? When will it ever be enough?"*

Sobbing, I then called out to Jenna, *"Can you hear me? Jenna, are you here? I need you. I can't do this anymore, Jenna. It hurts, and I don't know what to do. It always hurts, and my heart is always in pain. Jenna, help me."*

Tears dropped from my cheeks, pooling on the carpet beneath me and discoloring it. My nose was blocked as I gasped for air between cries. My body rocked back and forth, attempting to soothe itself.

Just as the crying and wailing increased, a sudden flush came over me. My entire body felt tingly, almost fuzzy, but from the inside.

The crying instantly stopped as I fell into a trance. My eyes closed, and although I was aware of my body, I simultaneously felt detached from it. The rocking turned into a gentle sway, and I saw a vision. I was in a field of flowers, completely surrounded.

They had long stems and large, bold petals. The flowers came about chest-high, and I stretched my arms out as they grazed my skin. There was a slight breeze, and even though it was daytime, there was no sun. The sky had a blurry, pale blue appearance, almost as if painted by an amateur artist.

I was at peace and happy. I felt light and airy, giggling as the flowers kissed my skin. I was teleported out of pain and into pleasure. I wanted to stay in that field.

I wanted to run and play through the flowers. I hoped that I had died and that this was heaven. This would be my new life. One of ease and joy.

The density of my depression evaporated, and I felt

relieved. I was weightless and harmonious amongst the flowers. There was no fear or sadness, no pain or anxiety. This must be what it's like to die. To no longer be bound to Earth, shackled by emotion and turmoil.

I joyously traipsed through the field. My laughter echoed but sounded more like a child than me. I'm not sure how long I was there, but eventually something told me it was time to return.

Fear swept over me because I didn't want to leave. I didn't want to leave this gorgeous field of flowers. I wanted this to be my new home.

Even though I tried to persuade the voice to let me stay, I gently returned to my body, fully present and aware as I remained sitting on the carpet in my bedroom.

I opened my eyes and looked around the room, hoping it would be the field, but disappointed when it wasn't.

I was reluctant to leave but I was okay being back in my bedroom. I was calm and tranquil. I got up off the floor, lay in my bed, and fell asleep.

From that point on, it felt a little easier forcing myself to get back to living. The darkness lost some of its strength, and I could go for a walk around the neighborhood or clean the house for thirty minutes.

Slowly but surely, I moved myself to a healthier place of being. Though it still hurt, and my heart still ached, the pain had dulled enough for me to begin living again. I was relieved.

It was true that a part of me wanted to be swallowed by the darkness, for it to be the excuse for why I died or at least spent my life barely surviving.

I'm not sure what that part of me is called, but it finds solace in suffering. Yet, the part of me that desires to heal and thrive was coming to the surface, proving to be my savior.

My life was slowly getting better, but I still felt restless. I wanted movement. I felt displaced. I no longer had any reason to stay in the US, but I wasn't sure where to go next.

I was at a familiar junction, the secluded intersection of endless possibilities and no idea which turn to take. I knew something needed to change, but I knew nothing more than that.

Part of me wanted to relocate to some obscure location where I could fade into the background. Maybe buy a condominium near a beach in Ecuador, Peru, Portugal, or Italy.

My traveler's feet were itching, but I remained hesitant to scratch them. I wondered if I was only trying to escape myself or if the desire to wander was genuine. Sometimes, it's hard to tell the difference.

While checking my email late one night, I came across a discount for a tarot reading. I recalled the accuracy of the woman in Nashville and how she predicted Jenna's death. My stomach tingled when I read the email, and I took action.

I jumped on the phone and called the number to see if they had anything to say. Maybe they could offer some insight into my desire to wander.

The woman I spoke to was nice. After going through the basics of name, date of birth, and specific desires, we got into the session.

She said a couple of things that were too open for interpretation. Things that were vague enough to be applicable in various circumstances. Things that aren't convincing enough for me like, *"You've been through a lot. You are feeling confused. I can see a better future."*

Who isn't any of those things? Who calls a psychic when life is going well and everything makes sense? I would need more to let down my guard. I want to be told something specific.

Just as I was calculating how much money I had lost from this call; she proceeded to tell me something of interest. A topic that I was careful not to divulge or inquire about. Something that would reveal if she was an authentic psychic. She told me a little about Jenna.

She said that Jenna was helping to guide children and that she was better in death than in life. It made me slightly sad, but I liked hearing it.

While Jenna was alive, I desperately wanted her to be better in life, but it was in vain. It was for my pleasure and desire, not for her or her destiny. Now, she was free to fulfill what was needed of her.

The woman went on to say that Jenna was with me and guiding me until I found my way, that she would stay until I figured out my path.

That was enough to activate my tear production, as they streamed down my cheeks, dropping on the pillow beneath me. I felt loved, but I also felt slightly guilty.

I wished the session was more of a three-way call. I wanted to ask Jenna questions and for her to ease my pain. I wanted Jenna to give me details and to show herself to me so that I could verify that she was safe.

I was left with a sense of unfulfillment as the psychic moved on to discuss my love life and her limited access due to spiritual blockages on my side. Every psychic I have seen has said the same thing. Entities on my side, guides, blocked most messages from being relayed.

After the session, we disconnected the call, and I remained still, thinking about what she had just said. Part of me wanted Jenna to stay with me forever. I wanted her with me all day long. Yet, another part of me wanted her to move on to her next adventure.

Her life on Earth had been sheltered and traumatic. I

wanted her to soar to other planets, dimensions, and universes. I wanted her to explore the skies and navigate her next journey with ease. I didn't want her to be stuck on Earth with me.

I felt heavyhearted that she was waiting for me. I needed to figure out what my own journey was so that Jenna could be free to move on. Where do I even start? I had no desire or passion for anything other than traveling.

I sat with myself for several days trying to figure out how to allow Jenna the freedom to move on. How to find my own way or path in life. What was I meant to do? What was Jenna waiting for me to discover? Nothing was coming to me.

I decided to stop trying to force it and instead allowed it to come to me in its own time. Perhaps I wasn't ready for my journey or the timing wasn't quite aligned just yet. I put it to the back of my mind and allowed myself the space to receive new opportunities or possibilities.

While online, browsing the headlines, I heard that a popular hike in Zion National Park, Utah, was going to switch to permit-only access. It would use the same lottery-style drawing as they did for The Wave. Since I had not visited this trail on my last trip, I decided to go back to Utah to hike it before the changeover.

The trail is called Angel's Landing, and it can be dangerous, as there have been fatalities along the trail. Over twenty deaths have been recorded since it opened in 1926. With an elevation incline of 1,500 feet, it was steep and intense.

Exactly what I was looking for. Something exciting to set my soul on fire. I wanted to again, feel small but also alive.

I wanted to clear my head and reset myself. The photos online made the hike look stunning, so I set off on another glorious Utah adventure.

Once in Zion, I made my way to the trail early in the morning. I was hoping to avoid the massive surge of hikers who were also trying to climb before permits began.

The hike itself took several hours, with numerous points that were narrow or required the use of chains to climb. People descending would patiently wait to pass at a safe spot.

Terror overcame me when we would have to pass at the edge of the cliff. I tried my best to regularly wipe the sweat from my hands for safer gripping.

I had never been on a hike that felt that dangerous before. My heart was pounding out of my chest the entire time, and I even started to hyperventilate toward the end of the climb. It was dizzying and intense.

I tried not to look down, but sometimes it was unavoidable. Twice in my life, I've wanted to kill myself by jumping off a balcony.

For some reason, that's always been the way I

imagined I would go. Here I was, scaling the side of a dangerous peak, nearly passing out from fear.

I realized that the darker aspect of myself fantasized about dying, but the primary aspect of myself wanted to live. I was so intensely afraid of falling at Angel's Landing that I could hardly breathe.

That petrifying fear made me realize something. I do, in fact, want to live. I was grateful that the darker parts of myself didn't win during my times of frailty. And in an odd way, I felt a sense of belonging. Perhaps I belong here, on Earth, for the time being.

As I made my way to the top, I sat down to catch my breath and absorb what had just happened. Tears rolled down my cheeks as I pondered the meaning of life, the purpose of my own existence.

My heart continued to race, but it was no longer out of fear. My elevated heart rate and tightening throat were from gratitude. They were from love.

They were aligned with the desire to live. To live on for as long as I could. To honor Jenna with my life and not my death.

The view from the top was spectacular, overlooking the entire canyon sprawling with rock formations and cliffs. The vegetation was lush with vibrant hues of green and tan.

I, once again, found myself pulling the sandwich bag

from my backpack, pinching some remains and sprinkling Jenna at the top of Angel's Landing.

I couldn't have imagined a better place for her. Not only the name but the location, the beauty. It also connected with a personal realization about life and death. It might have been the perfect place for all her ashes but I was far too greedy for that.

I always think about Jenna when I visit national parks. Her love of plants and gardens would have thrived in places like these. I once saw a job opening for a park ranger during the summer. I sent her the link in an attempt to get her to try something new.

I thought it would have been an amazing experience, her learning about new species of plants and connecting with like-minded people, spending the summer living at the park and seeing where life would take her.

She had already been struggling with addiction at that point, though I didn't know about it yet. I got annoyed when she turned the opportunity down, talking herself out of the experience.

I hated how secluded her life was, always staying with Cain and never venturing far from his house. She missed out on everything life had to offer.

I sometimes wonder how amazing it would have been if she had become a park ranger. How many interesting stories she would have amassed, and how much knowledge she would have gained.

I could have visited her and seen her dressed in her official uniform. Sometimes, when I close my eyes, I imagine it.

I found myself scrolling on Craigslist, late one night. I love that website and have found some amazing things on it. I came across an advertisement for an addiction recovery coaching certification. I clicked through, visited the site, and inquired about the course. I ended up enrolling in the nine-month program.

Each week, you attend two video sessions and complete an online course section. You move through the program at your own pace, meaning if you stop completing the online work or stop attending the video sessions, it stretches out the course. However, if you complete everything on time, you finish in nine months.

Initially, nine months felt like a long time; however, the course went quickly, and I finished on time. I learned a lot about addiction, including the addiction cycle, triggers, relapse, helpful strategies for those in addiction, boundary setting, enabling, and much more.

It was very insightful. It was a little too densely connected to AA, which I thought wasn't the best approach. Other than that, I enjoyed it and was glad to have completed the course and gotten certified as an addiction recovery coach.

During my months of study, I began to find bird feathers. They were usually gray and varied in size. Some were tiny, while others were longer than my hand. Each time a feather crossed my path, I picked it up and examined it.

I assigned the feathers a meaning. These were gifts from Jenna, her way of dropping in to say hello and let me know I was on the right path. A little motivation and love.

I kept all the feathers I found and placed them on a shelf in the kitchen. It's a shelf dedicated to Jenna and her remembrance.

Just like the helium balloons I only ever found immediately after Jenna's death; the feathers only appeared during my addiction recovery coaching course.

I was beginning to rediscover who I used to be before Jenna's death. The old parts of me, those that were happy and calm, were starting to return, though I was not entirely the same. Nonetheless, I was pleased to see those old parts again.

I had extensively detached from myself in every way once learning about her addiction. I was so far separated from the person I knew that I didn't think it was possible to return. I assumed I would be permanently different. I had changed, how could I not. Yet, these changes were proving to be an internal metamorphosis.

To be perfectly honest, though, there was still a lingering sense of grief and I remained easily angered. Levels of frustration at insignificant things or events still resided within. It was milder, but it was there. I couldn't always control it, and the smallest things would still set me off.

The grief had left my nervous system overstimulated and the remnants remained. Almost as if I had carved out a new pattern of behavior. It was hard to shift. I felt myself defaulting straight to annoyance without a pause.

It was as though a slow driver was the biggest inconvenience in the world. As if a car that cut me off in traffic wanted to incite a war. I felt vulnerable and lashed out externally in an attempt to protect that part of me.

I didn't like that about myself. It was considerably different from my state of being before Jenna's death. It felt like a stranger was popping up within me each time it occurred. I felt ashamed and embarrassed by my immature reactions.

I read that these types of behaviors can sometimes be associated with depression, too. While I wasn't feeling the intense depression I usually know, it was possible that I was depressed to a lesser degree, almost at a functional level.

I only ever call it depression when I feel debilitated and unable to move from the bed or take a shower. To think that depression could be more widespread in my life was

Amanda Bourque

discouraging.

To be fair, it would be absurd to expect myself to fully recover from Jenna's death after a couple of years. I had spent my entire life with her. I never had a memory of life without her.

That isn't something you heal from in a short amount of time. It might be something I never fully heal from. How could I, really?

I tried my best to be patient with myself but also proactive. It was a possibility that I would internalize some level of grief for the rest of my life.

I was at peace with that. What I was not at peace with was my reaction to external events or circumstances. There was no reason to revert to childlike behaviors because there was traffic or a long line at the grocery store.

I had to undo the pattern that formed from my grief. I had to consciously choose to respond in a way that better aligned with who I wanted to be. I had to remove myself from the lingering grip of anger.

It was not easy for me to do, and it is a continuous process I'm not always successful at. Some days are better than others. Some situations are easier than others.

Whether I am succeeding or failing, I am trying. I try my best in each moment, and that's all I can ever do. Hopefully, it fades and eventually becomes a part of me that I

~ 290 ~

no longer remember.

The hardest times are around Christmas. I often reflect on our childhood memories and what the holidays might look like if Jenna were still alive. From Christmas and New Years to the anniversary of her death and her birthday, it's exactly two months.

It's a difficult block of time to get through. I often feel a wide array of emotions and find myself retreating to my safe haven, the bed. A time when everyone seems to ask what you did for the holidays but I chock back the truth.

I still hide my pain because there is nothing anyone can do to soothe it. It's part of me and I surrender to its depths, accepting my new normal.

As I reflected on my coaching course, I couldn't help but compare what I learned to my experience with Jenna. When I was going through everything with her, there were a lot of things I didn't understand.

Perhaps I was too caught up with her and unable to see clearly. Or I was just unaware of what I didn't know.

Aspects such as the addiction cycle, enabling, and how to support sobriety. There were so many things that I wished I knew while she was alive. I regretted learning about them when it was too late. Too late to benefit her, anyway.

A desire to continue learning rumbled within. There was more here that I needed to explore, so I enrolled in a separate online program to become a certified life coach and later took an additional sobriety coaching course.

It seemed to spiral and take on a life of its own, all the information I was studying and the people I was meeting. I was being challenged to make actionable moves in the direction of addiction recovery and coaching others.

While out on an evening walk, the idea of volunteering at a rehabilitation center popped into my mind. The following day, I called several centers and eventually found one. The position was to facilitate group meetings twice a week, two hours each day.

I understood the family perspective on addiction, the fears, struggles, and misguided actions. I did not, however, have the perspective of an addict. This volunteer position would help fill that gap.

I could take everything I had learned and merge it with everything I had experienced, then package it to illuminate the journey for others. It was starting to make sense. My pain, did in fact, have a purpose. Or, at the very least, I could turn it into a purpose.

It felt easy to move in this direction, so easy, in fact, that I knew it was aligned with something greater than me, a source of energy guiding me into this space. To serve others and give meaning to not only my strife, but to theirs as well.

Working with the addicts at the treatment center

taught me a lot, not only about addiction but also about the pain behind it. Each one of them had endured a difficult life, whether they openly admitted it or not. It didn't take many stories to get a sense of what their lives had been like.

Some of their stories were extremely difficult to hear. When they shared their experiences, being raped, abused, neglected, disowned, manipulated, it was difficult to listen.

It was as though these stories of suffering were at the surface the entire time. Just waiting for the moment they could be released. I held space for them regardless of how uncomfortable it was.

It reminded me of when I reached out to a counselor during my year of rage. How it was met with emptiness and how that only drove me to deeper isolation and desperation. I didn't want to be like her. I wasn't going to let these stories fall to the floor unnoticed.

One woman shared that she had been raped and passed around to neighbors and relatives from the age of four. I had to choke back tears as she cried, looking me in the eye while she spoke. The bravery she possessed to speak about this in front of a room full of people left me in awe.

Or men breaking down into tears as they talked about how they almost killed themselves before entering the rehabilitation center. About the girlfriends, spouses and parents who had died in tragic ways. No wonder they wanted to escape. No wonder they needed to numb themselves.

Story after story of hardship, war, murder, gangs, family affiliations, attempted suicides, and rejection. No matter what things they may have done, I felt sad for them. I wished life had been different for them.

Sometimes it feels as though the weight of the world perpetually presses down on you, and there is no end to the pain and inner torment. I could relate to their darkness on many levels. Sometimes I would think about them for days, wondering how they even survived.

Being at the rehabilitation center gave me a compassion towards addiction that I never had before. During my year of anger following Jenna's death, I was out late one night.

I had to be up early the following morning and needed gas, so I figured I'd get some on the way home. I stopped at a station, got gas, and decided to take the back roads.

As soon as I rounded the corner from the gas station, I saw something lying on the sidewalk. Two bodies intertwined. The way they were twisted and folded together looked as though they were dead.

Even if they were homeless and sleeping on the street, no one would lie in such an awkward position. It almost appeared that their limbs would have to be broken to contort like that.

I slowed the car and rolled down the window. *Were they dead?* I wasn't about to get out of my car at 11 o'clock at night to check on them, so I did the next best thing.

"Hey! You alive? Hey! Hello?" I shouted.

There was no answer, but I could see at least one of them breathing. I thought about calling 911. They were definitely on drugs, maybe overdosing. Any addict will tell you they want to die.

At least that's what Jenna used to tell me, that it feels so good when you overdose. Supposedly, she had been revived a few times and was angry each time she was brought back to life.

Maybe these two people, lying intertwined on the sidewalk, also wanted the same thing. If they wanted to die, who was I to call the police? They were just junkies. Let them die. Let them waste their lives. Let them face whatever entity comes after death.

I rolled the window back up and continued home, wondering how many strangers had looked at my sweet, innocent Jenna the same way.

How many people had called her a dirty junkie and refused her help? How many had looked down on her and her beautiful curly hair?

I burst into tears before I reached my driveway. I suppose a lot of people looked at her that way. Who could blame them? There were many times I also looked at her that way.

I figured I'd check the news tomorrow to see if a couple was found dead by the gas station, but I never checked. And I never felt guilty about letting them face the consequences of their own actions.

I view things differently now, after being at the rehabilitation center. They are not dirty junkies or lost causes. They are people who have had a difficult life and made a choice, a choice made in desperation, a vain attempt to self-soothe and disappear, if only for a short time.

We have all tried to escape before, whether through a few glasses of wine or the whole bottle, a late-night binge on carbohydrates or sex with a stranger. Perhaps it's a run on the treadmill, or an intense weightlifting session.

Others try to drown themselves in work or overconsume and rack up credit card debt from excessive shopping. There are many who use video games to escape reality, even inventing their own virtual world.

Some overmedicate, while others use and abuse people to escape from themselves. We all do it. It's just that some of us do it in socially acceptable ways.

The differences may seem vast, but the degrees of separation are not as wide as we think. If you had made a different decision, if you had turned right instead of left, tried cocaine instead of beer, been in a different friend group, or had a different home life. One tiny pebble could have made any of us something completely different.

The more I spoke with the people at the center, the more I understood addiction, the shame it brings, how it consumes the mind, and how it ruins lives. Most of them had little to no family left. Some had been introduced to drugs by their parents, which was shocking and upsetting to hear, as it angered me.

Listening their stories of how their families continuously drew them back into dysfunction and relapse broke my heart. The cycles of enabling and failed sobriety attempts mirrored Jenna's relationship with Cain. Some people are so distorted that they would rather someone die than change. I still struggle to understand that.

For my initial addiction recovery coaching course, we were required to read several books. One book, in particular, spoke directly to this issue.

The author used the example of a husband and wife. The wife was an alcoholic, and the husband claimed he wanted her to stop drinking and get help.

She entered treatment and was doing well. But after a short time, back home, the husband began isolating her. He kept bottles of alcohol around the house, initiated fights, prevented her from attending AA meetings, and even asked her to go buy beer for him.

The husband was sabotaging her recovery. He said he wanted her to stop drinking, but when she returned sober, he realized something, her sobriety meant he would also need to change.

The household would need to function differently and that's when he began to sabotage her. Preventing her from attending meetings, making sober friends and altering their relationship dynamic.

Even though the husband claimed that he wanted his wife to get sober, he wanted it to be on his own terms. He wanted to maintain control over the relationship and prevent her from ever leaving. He was unwilling to change alongside her.

In reality, it never mattered how much Mother Mary and I did for Jenna. It didn't matter what we tried to do to get her help or to reach her. As long as Cain was attached to her, there was no way we could have gotten through to her.

Cain acted just like the husband in the book. Toxic family members will only identify with the version of you they have the most power over. Happily trading health for malady.

The hardest aspect of working at the rehabilitation center was seeing those who relapsed. It was never a surprise. You could tell who was genuinely trying to change and who wasn't, who was ready to leave the addiction cycle and who was still stuck in the darkness.

It's interesting that addicts will go to rehab before they are truly ready to get sober. Sometimes, I think it's because they're trying to avoid certain consequences, whether from family or the law. Other times, they underestimate how drastically their lives need to change to maintain sobriety.

It's overwhelming and can feel isolating. They have to fully surrender to the process, but not everyone entering rehab is willing to do that. I even heard stories of some people going to five or six different treatment centers in a year.

While it's true that I don't know the depth of addiction, I do know the depth of despair. I can relate on that level. I can empathize with strife. My life has not been easy at all. I have been through darkness myself and know its magnitude.

I have had devilish words spoken into my head that reverberated and echoed loudly for years. I could understand how they might straddle between addiction and sobriety.

A lot of the people I interacted with at the center are kind, caring, and beam with light. I can't help but wonder why they even had to turn to substances.

They seem too gentle for that type of life. I guess that's a trait that Jenna shares with them: too sensitive, too gentle, too empathic, and too caring for the coldness of this world.

Jenna would have turned out sweeter if things were different.

I think I will always wonder how Jenna would have turned out if we had come from a good home, if the circumstances had been different. I don't ever wonder how I would have turned out differently, but I do wonder about Jenna.

It seems like such a waste of a life. She never moved out of Cain's house. She never went to college. She never traveled. She never saw a sliver of what was possible in life. I hate that so much.

I often have to remind myself that life is not for me to dictate, nor is it for me to concoct an alternate ending for anyone. Each person is in control of themselves. They can do whatever they like with their life.

They can live with their nose in the dirt, or they can dance on the moon. We are the ones who either limit ourselves or propel ourselves.

As time goes on, I think of Jenna less and less. I used to feel guilty for that, but I don't anymore. Life goes on, and I also have to go on. If I were to think about her, I would get sad, and I cannot live my life like that.

It's almost as though I have compartmentalized Jenna and her death. That reality exists, but it's in a very small part of my subconscious. It's tucked away in the back and doesn't interfere with my daily activities. I have to do that. I love her too much to live any other way.

I sometimes feel as though she exists in the world. She's somewhere, not too far from Cain's house, getting into some kind of mischief or being dramatic about something or another.

In general, though, her spiritual presence is much less. I think it's close to being completely gone.

Perhaps she hung around so that I could heal, so she could comfort me and send me messages. Maybe I've found my way through the darkness, and she is free to go on to the next adventure.

As the eldest, I always thought I was responsible for carving out paths and making a way for her, even though I was never successful in getting her to follow me when she was alive. The roles may be switched now.

It's my turn to have her carve a path for me. My job is to live and fulfill my purpose until it's time to leave.

I can only hope that it's Jenna who meets me once this life is over. There is no one else I would prefer. She could show me around and tell me about all the shortcuts she's discovered to make the transition easier and more fun.

I always wondered why Jenna never followed me as a role model. If this is my opportunity to reverse the roles, I want to make sure that I do follow her. I would love to follow her through to the next adventure.

CHAPTER SIXTEEN

.·.

"There will come a time when you believe everything is finished. That will be the beginning."

Louis L'Amour

I can now look back on the entire experience differently. I can see what worked and what didn't. I can see where the gaps were and where we faltered with Jenna. If I had the opportunity to do everything over again, I would change many things.

When I meet people who are currently struggling with a family member's addiction, I am able to offer them my insight and experience. I can contribute to making them feel less alone.

It's through hardships and tribulations that we bring

insight and substance to others. I use my mistakes as a launching point to provide comfort, knowledge and solace to others who have or are going through similar experiences.

The turmoil that families endure is expansive and often overlooked. They are forced into situations that they never wanted to be in. Situations that make them choose between themselves and their loved one. How do you even make that choice?

How are families supposed to suffer in the background, in the shadows, and endlessly withstand the pain associated with watching someone with an addiction?

Many of whom hold onto their distress for fear of being exposed. For the family secret to be revealed, for their failures to come to light, for their disdain to be unveiled.

Whenever I seek out advice from others I usually want to know where they went wrong. I want to know about their regrets or what they wish they knew sooner.

So, when I reflect on everything that happened with Jenna, I am able to clearly see what mistakes were made and what I would have liked someone to tell me about addiction.

If I could do things over, I would have checked in with her more. Even though Jenna was always reserved, I would have made an attempt to approach her differently.

I would have taken more time to establish better communication with her, attempting to have more collaborative dialogue with her.

My communication has always been blunt and aggressive. She never liked it, and I never tried to change it to accommodate her. Learning to communicate with various types of people is an important life skill. I ignored that.

I would have participated more in activities that she enjoyed. I would have explored more hobbies alongside her, rather than just sending her off to do those things alone. I would have made an effort to take joy in dual participation.

It could have been a bonding and trust-building opportunity for us. Maybe that meant learning about gardening or how to strum the guitar.

I would have taken her interests and made them my own curiosities. I never made much of an effort in that aspect of our relationship. Instead, I always wanted her to join my interests.

I never would have forced myself onto Jenna when I first found out about her addiction. We were very forceful and aggressive. We attempted to mandate that Jenna get into a rehabilitation center and tried to become an authority over her.

This pushed her away and gave her a reason to self-isolate. It was also a wonderful excuse for her to lean into Cain more. Which is exactly what he wanted.

No one likes to be forced into anything, adults and

children alike. I'm not sure why we thought that was the best response. It felt like it came from a place of fear rather than helpfulness.

We were consumed by the fear of losing her and the pain associated with it. It also led nowhere and was extremely exhausting to maintain. We made it about us rather than her.

The desperation from the fear of her dying overruled and turned us into authoritarians. That approach never works. I've since heard countless stories about families attempting to force or coerce their loved ones into treatment.

No one changes because they were forced to. No matter how difficult that is to accept, it's the truth. Even though we are afraid for them and what might happen, the desire must come from them because they must do the work.

There are things we can do to assist them, support them, guide them, or even encourage them. However, force will never achieve the desired results.

I remember the first time Jenna told me that she had taken oxycodone, we were teenagers. It was within the first seven to ten months after I left Mother Mary's house.

Jenna and I were at Cain's house, she pulled me aside and told me that a boyfriend of Cain's second family had given it to her. She smirked as she explained that it was similar to heroin, almost as if she were proud.

I stood there in disbelief at both her smirk and her

words. I initially thought she was joking or trying to get a rise out of me. After a small amount of inquiry, I found out it was true.

I pulled her supplier aside and threatened him. I never said anything to Cain or Mother Mary. Even though Jenna was young, we all experimented with drugs. I didn't want to get her in trouble if it was minor or a one-time thing.

Many people who use opioids describe it as a quieting of the mind. After many years of intense and intrusive inner thoughts, opioids bring calm and silence. They can finally rest and relax mentally.

Since I walked away from my childhood with those types of inner thoughts, I'm sure Jenna did as well. She never discussed it with me. She hardly discussed anything of substance, but I can assume that's what drew her to drugs and ultimately opioids.

Though I also wonder how she decided to try opioids right away. She was young when she first tried them. I could only assume that it was because she had a connection that was in the same house.

Cain's house was always filled with strange characters, and getting your hands on drugs was easy. I wonder if she was pressured. She certainly fantasized about heroin from a young age. I wonder if she knew someone who did it and idolized them. I have a few possibilities in my mind.

If I could go back and do everything over, I would have made a big deal about her taking oxycodone. Actually, I would have caused hell about it. I would have run to Mother Mary. I would have run to Cain. I would have called the police.

Sometimes you let things slide because you hope they aren't a big deal or because you might look foolish otherwise. As her older sister, I thought one instance wasn't serious.

However, it was a pivotal moment in Jenna's life. It was the moment she started down the path of addiction. Something that once seemed insignificant now revealed itself as substantial.

I wish I had taken the risk and looked like a fool. I wish I had scooped Jenna up at that very moment and never allowed her to return to Cain's house, because that was the very moment she got sucked into the darkness.

I also think that we should have hired a professional to help orchestrate an intervention once we found out about her addiction. The best time to intervene is during the remorse phase of the addiction cycle. We could have worked with a professional to recognize this phase and get Jenna into treatment.

A professional also could have offered us the guidance and support we desperately needed at that time. It would have saved us from trying to figure things out on our own and failing at every turn. Instead, efforts could have been directed in a more efficient manner.

Going back, I wish I understood that addiction is called a family disease because it affects the entire family. It also requires that the entire family participate in the recovery process. While this is not always possible, as with Cain, I would have tried to compensate for him anyway.

Instead of shuffling Jenna off to fix the issue on her own, I wish I understood that she needed the support of all of us to change alongside her. I used to think that the addiction was her problem. Now I understand that she needed all of us in order to be successful in sobriety.

I wish I understood to be more compassionate towards her. I thought that it was her wrong that she needed to go make right. I assumed it was a minor bump rather than the life-long sentence it actually is. I downplayed the severity of her problems because I had never had the same ones.

As with the story of the husband with the alcoholic wife, dysfunctional relationships are impossible to continue for an addict in recovery.   Their entire life has to change. I never knew that, and I wish I had. I wish I had understood the severity of Jenna's relationship with Cain and its impact on her addiction.

I wish I understood that Cain would forever lure Jenna back into suffering. He never released her from his grasp, and he never had any intentions to.

Almost like wedding vows, it was until death do them part. I wish I had researched codependency and addiction. I wish I knew what codependency was.

You never think that family could be the cause, or the continuous cause, of your problems, but it absolutely can be. Not to say that anyone is bad or evil, but people are ignorant and cope in particular ways.

I don't believe Cain consciously wanted Jenna to be addicted, but he definitely did on a subconscious level. I knew he was dysfunctional, but I had no understanding of the power of that dysfunction.

This might not be surprising, but he still continues to exhibit the same patterns and behaviors. He will never change because he has no desire to.

He doesn't see the magnificent destruction of his actions. Just as we couldn't convince Jenna to change, no one can convince Cain to change.

The only time an individual does inner work is when they choose to. Each one of us is flawed and imperfect, yet it's only those with personal awareness who understand this.

We all have to advocate for ourselves and set boundaries, even with family members. I wish I understood boundaries more and how vital they are to healthy relationships. It's difficult to know what they are or how to implement them if you come from a dysfunctional family.

I wish I had learned more about healthy boundaries and practiced it, not only for my own relationships but also to understand the negative consequences of not having boundaries.

This would have helped me most when I was growing weary of Jenna's active addiction. When I was having the recurring nightmare, and she was trampling all over me.

That being said, I also would have done more to separate Jenna and Cain. I'm not exactly sure what I would have done, but I should have done more.

Whether through the assistance of professionals, the police, or strategic sabotage, I wish I had ripped those two apart from the beginning. He was the main reason Jenna never got better.

Jenna did go to rehab several times, yet when she finished, she would run back to Cain's house. How could anyone expect to maintain change in a toxic environment?

Every rehabilitation program teaches that you must remove yourself from old people, places, and things. It's the only way to maintain change, especially during the first year or two of recovery.

Jenna never even gave herself a chance at being sober. She was too attached to Cain to leave his side. They were obsessed with each other. I wish I had understood how vital an individual's environment is to their recovery.

Every single person connected to the addict must be willing to either change or distance themselves. This offers the opportunity for sobriety and a stable new life. The person addicted must be the enforcer and maintainer of this.

I did attend several Al-Anon meetings when Jenna was active in her addiction. Since they didn't align with me, I abandoned them. If I could do things again, I would have found an alternative support group, one that felt more actionable and productive for my personal needs.

I was unaware of alternative resources and assumed all support groups were the same. I wish I had investigated that option more. It would have helped me manage Jenna and regulate myself.

I have spoken a lot about what I would have done differently, but what about what I would have done the same? What would I have done one hundred times over if I could?

It's sometimes easier to focus on the regrets, but I think it's important to highlight the things that I was content with, even after Jenna's death.

I would have distanced myself from Jenna again. Perhaps I would have done it sooner. I needed to separate myself from her because she was dragging me into her darkness, just as Cain had done to her, and Mother Mary had done to both Jenna and me.

Since darkness is familiar, I am highly susceptible to

its lure. Not everyone is like this, but I am. I don't regret doing it. Not for an instant. Even when Mother Mary threw it in my face at Jenna's funeral. I made the right decision for myself. I wish I didn't have to make that decision, but I did, and I honored myself with it.

Especially when you speak with professional interventionists, they all say the same thing: the person addicted must lose nearly everything as a consequence of rejecting rehab. All family members must be aligned with it and willing to enforce strict rules.

An addict must hit their bottom before they are willing to get help. When the family removes themselves, it makes the addict's life miserable. It forces a situation of despair that is needed for the addict to eventually seek help.

I did the right thing by removing myself. It would have worked if Cain and Mother Mary had joined me. However, they were too selfish and weak to do the only productive thing we could have done. They thought more about their own pain than Jenna's. They refused to sacrifice that in order to get Jenna help.

In reality, it never mattered that Mother Mary tried to make me feel bad about it. She wanted me to feel guilty about doing something that she was incapable of doing.

She wanted me to feel like the selfish one. I was always the bad one. Yet, we both knew that she was, in fact, the callous one.

I undoubtedly would have hosted Jenna at my house to detox many times over. It was an opportunity for her to get sober and for me to get through to her.

Though both times were not successful, I made the attempt and would do it again. I would change a few things, but I would have still had her detox with me at least once.

I made the right decision by staying in the US, especially during her active addiction. I also made the right choice to continue to stay after separating myself from Jenna. Being only a few hours away by plane was useful on several occasions, even after Jenna died.

It was one of the biggest sacrifices I made for her, but I would have done it many times again if I could. That's what sisters do for each other. They do their best to support and help in whatever ways possible.

I have since returned to visit India, but I didn't go to Hampi. It seems like a lifetime ago or perhaps it was just a dream. A fantasy place that my subconscious created in an attempt to fill a void. If it was nothing but a dream, I prefer to keep it secured, safely in my heart.

When it came to Jenna's sobriety, we failed miserably. There's no disputing that. Though, not for a lack of trying. However, I would have put the same amount of determination into trying to save her. A lot of our efforts were misguided, ignorant, or based on fear. Yet, we tried the very best we could during that time.

None of us really knew anything about addiction and were throwing punches while blindfolded, hoping that eventually one of them would land.

I would have expelled all the energy, hope, and possibilities out of myself all over again. That was the right thing to do for me and our situation. I have no regrets about that.

I can connect my leaving Mother Mary's house with Jenna's opioid usage. I know the two were intertwined. It hurts that they were, but it was the reality of it. I was no longer there to protect Jenna, and I no longer was there to monitor her wellness.

Even though that was the case, I would have left again. I had to choose my life in that instance, and it was the right decision. I wish I was never forced to be in that position, but I was. I wish I wasn't made to abandon Jenna, but I was.

I feel as though I sacrificed a large portion of my life for Jenna. I left India, stayed in the US, endured the turmoil, faded into darkness, and nearly took my own life.

Despite that, I would do it all over again if I could. There isn't a molecule within my body that wouldn't do it all over again. In fact, I would have gone harder and given more of myself for her.

Reflecting back can sometimes be overwhelming. The pressure I put on myself to be some sort of supreme version of a sister. A person who knows everything and responds perfectly at every moment.

I was being far too harsh on myself. Expecting perfection through-and-through. I was also punishing myself for the way life turned out for Jenna.

No one knows what is ahead. None of us know just how fragile life is until we find ourselves in the midst of chaos and possible loss. It's just how life works.

While the future is unpredictable, our own tenacity and perseverance are what guide us through. Having faith in the fact that whatever happens, it will be okay, whether we like what happened or not. It will be okay. Life will continue, and we will move on.

Being the sister of an addict is not easy. We often find ourselves alone and invisible. Our needs are forgotten about or considered unimportant. It's frustrating, confusing, and devastating. We can sometimes even be cast out of the family because of this. No matter what, we remain sisters, and nothing can ever change that.

My life has been permanently altered. I will never be the same, and that's okay. I will, however, go on to fulfill my life and its purpose. I will move through any hardships with strength and determination.

I will make my sister proud, no matter where she is or whether she can see me. My sister lives on as long as I live on. We are forever connected and forever intertwined.

I still wear the fingerprint necklace nearly every day. Even though the memory of Jenna is dulled and resides in the back of my mind, the necklace keeps her essence at the forefront.

Each time I put it on, there is a glimmer of her. Each time I look in the mirror, I can have a moment for her. Each time I take it off at night, I am comforted by her.

From time to time, I think about what the psychic said. I wonder if Jenna is floating through the universe or dimensions, assisting children. I get a tinge of jealousy in those moments. I, too, want to be in another dimension, to be finished with the physical world and drift through space.

There are nights when the lore draws me in and I fantasize about dying as I drift off to sleep. I imagine that I will never wake up again, that I am free, joyous and at peace. I am with Jenna once again and we are dancing in a field of flowers.

The next morning, disappointment sinks in my stomach as I realize it's not yet my time. An older sister that is jealous of her younger sibling. It's a secret feeling that us elders keep. It's certainly more common than one might assume.

It took a while before I felt ready to talk about Jenna to others. Each time I tried, a knot would form in my throat. It prevented me from sharing my story.

My eyes would fill with tears just thinking about saying a few words or two. The reality that I would have to speak her name in the same sentence as *"died, dead"* or *"passed away,"* was confronting.

It was as if each time was a resurrection of her death, and the pain associated with it. I avoided her and our story in an attempt to evade the discomfort. As if that would make it less real.

Keeping Jenna quiet and locked away would be a disservice to her. Like with her ashes, my role now is to spread her throughout the world.

My experience with Jenna connects me to millions of other people who have similar plights. I am not alone in this pain; I know that.

As I get better at sharing the story of Jenna to others, more people migrate toward me. People who share similar stories, people who have similar pain, and people who need support. It's become a beacon which has given me the opportunity to better connect families with their addicted loved ones.

Even though speaking about Jenna is still sometimes difficult, I am able to offer more than sad eyes to those who struggle. I can provide valuable insight and perspective because of Jenna.

I believe in my heart that this is the direction that she has guided me to. I must be strong for her, for myself, and for everyone else who struggles.

A friend invited me to a community yoga class. It was outdoors along a river. I excitedly accepted and arrived early to claim our spots.

I found the perfect place and laid down my mat. Sitting down, crossed-legged I began to stretch to warm up. My eyes glanced to the right and instantly fixated on an object.

It was something silver. I reached out and picked it up. On single silver heart earring. I thought about Jenna and all the heart shapes I found immediately following her death.

I smiled and kept the thought of her with me the entire class. Once it was over, we rolled up our mats and made our way to a coffee shop. For some reason my gaze moved down and in that same moment a small grey feather glided in and settled on the ground by my feet.

I picked it up and held it close to my heart. This has to be Jenna. Maybe she's leaving. Maybe I'm good now. Maybe I've truly found my way. I brought both objects back home and placed them the shelf in the kitchen.

I had to make an emergency visit to the dentist. Not a

place I love to be and especially when it's urgent.

Upon examining me he asked, *"Do you grind or clench your teeth at all?"*

"Grind my teeth? Absolutely not," I quickly responded, almost insulted by the suggestion. And then I thought about it for a moment. It was true. Why had this not been something that I admitted to until now?

Sometime after Jenna's death I started clenching my jaw. I would wake several times a night, noticing it. Some nights were more than others and some weeks I wouldn't notice it at all.

It also started happening during the day as well with a slight soreness in my jaw from the pressure. I would catch myself doing it in the car, while on the computer or even while watching movies.

Unfortunately, it was something that I still did. Actually, I did it last night. I noticed it but didn't acknowledge it. Could that be denial or just ignoring my personal needs?

The dentist told me that it's stress related and to meditate, exercise or seek professional services. He also said that I would need to have a couple fillings redone as they were damaged from the clenching.

Remembering when it all began brought sadness to my heart. The very last physical remnants of Jenna's death linger and need to be addressed.

It was the clenching and the volatility. Perhaps they are intertwined. Nonetheless, I am actively trying to resolve both these issues. That small piece of me that wants Jenna with me forever feels conflicted about it.

Letting go completely has been more of a challenge than I anticipated. I want to move on so that she can be free. Yet, I can't help but selfishly desire her presence until my life ends. Moving on and continuing my life has been a battle.

I'm doing my best and trying to maintain some perspective on life, as a whole. Realizing that it goes quickly, and I still have more to do. Also extending this same sentiment to Jenna and whatever her next mission is.

As I continue on my journey as an addiction recovery coach, I find it to be fulfilling. I've never been drawn to any type of occupation. The only passion I've ever had was to travel and immerse myself in the lifestyle of others.

For the first time in my life, I feel as though I have a purpose, a path. It's the first time that my life made sense. As though all the fragmented pieces really do come back together to form a complete image.

The clients I work with are seeking answers. They are confused, exhausted, afraid, and isolated. I have the honor of shining light along their path. I have the privilege of offering insight, advice, information, compassion, and guidance to them.

I can fill the gaps that I, myself, needed filled during similar times. I've made it my mission to never give anyone sad eyes and a closed mouth.

I can share my message with anyone who is open to receiving it. I can offer actionable steps and guide people away from things that don't make an impact.

I never expected my life to turn in this direction. I never would have imagined that this would be where I would go. However, it's where Jenna has led me. I can now follow her lead. I can now allow her to carve out a path for me to follow.

I opened Facebook to browse the marketplace when I noticed a banner with recent friend requests. I only ever use Facebook for the marketplace, but the first request caught my eye. It was a name I recognized, my biological father's name, but this was his junior.

My father had a son with another woman when I was a teenager. I had met my half-brother once when he was just a baby.

Over the years, I sometimes wondered what he looked like. However, the truth is, I never thought he would ever find out about me.

Even though I only met my father a couple of times, when I initially left Mother Mary's house, I looked up his number and gave him a call. I had no place to stay and was about to spend my first night homeless in the woods. When I spoke to him, I hinted at the possibility of living with him.

All he wanted to do was give me money, and when I refused, he offered to rent me a studio apartment in New Hampshire. I was only sixteen and didn't want my own apartment any more than I wanted his money.

He eventually agreed to let me come to his house in Connecticut. I bought a Greyhound bus ticket and made the journey. I stayed there for two weeks.

Unfortunately, his new wife didn't like me, and she ended up sabotaging me. It was enough to convince my father to drive me back to New Hampshire, where he dropped me off outside a police station.

All I ever wanted was to be loved, yet he only wanted to continue like normal with his new family. I hated him for betraying me when I reached out for help. I hated him for not loving me.

It eventually ended in a shout-out with my father disowning me and my abused-child angst. I was just a teen, and I never heard from him again.

I always imagined that my brother, Junior would never know about me, the teenage mistake my father made and a long-lost secret. Well, a long-forgotten secret.

I immediately accepted the friend request and messaged him. *"Do we know each other?"* I wrote.

"No, we've never met. I think you're my half-sister though," Junior replied.

"Sister" that's a word I thought had died alongside Jenna. I never thought I'd be called a sister again. I read the message several times before bursting into tears.

I am a sister. I am still a sister. I am a reborn big sister. Is this a dream? Is this real? I rub my eyes and shake my shoulders to check. Yes, this is real.

ABOUT THE AUTHOR

Amanda Bourque is a certified addiction recovery coach and certified life coach who combines these unique skill sets to support people who suffer from addiction with an emphasis on their family and loved ones. *Living in My Sister's Shadow* is Amanda's debut novel and a memoir chronicling her and her sister's true life stories.

After studying business management at Southern New Hampshire University and graduating summa cum laude, she founded her own addiction recovery coaching service, Sober and Beyond, in honor of her beloved sister, Jenna. Amanda also frequently volunteers at an addiction rehabilitation center, which has helped her better understand her addicts' struggles and mindsets, making her a more effective resource for their recovery journeys.

After enduring many personal ordeals, Amanda is now determined to live her life to the fullest and help others along the way. She has pursued her passion for travel all her adult life and even spent five years living overseas, including in India, her favorite destination. She loves planning her next adventure abroad, reconnecting with nature, and taking annual hiking trips in Utah. She currently resides in Tampa,

Florida.

For more information about Amanda, her mission, and overcoming addiction, please visit her website at: www.soberandbeyond.com